HOW DO YOU
WANT ME?

RUBY WAX

HOW DO YOU WANT ME?

EBURY
PRESS

First published in Great Britain in 2002

1 3 5 7 9 10 8 6 4 2

Text © Ruby Wax 2002
Photographs © Ruby Wax unless otherwise credited

First published by
Ebury Press
Random House, 20 Vauxhall Bridge Road, London SW1V 2SA

Random House Australia (Pty) Limited
20 Alfred Street, Milsons Point, Sydney, New South Wales 2061, Australia

Random House New Zealand Limited
18 Poland Road, Glenfield, Auckland 10, New Zealand

Random House South Africa (Pty) Limited
Endulini, 5A Jubilee Road, Parktown 2193, South Africa

The Random House Group Limited Reg. No. 954009

www.randomhouse.co.uk

A CIP catalogue record for this book is available from the British Library.

Typeset by seagulls
Cover design by the Senate

ISBN 0091886627

Papers used by Ebury Press are natural, recyclable products
made from wood grown in sustainable forests.

Printed and bound in Great Britain by Clays Ltd., St Ives plc

ACKNOWLEDGEMENTS

I'd like to thank:
Ed for sticking around
Max, Maddy and Marina
All the Alans in my life
My friends ... You know who you are
Alison for unscrambling a confused mind.

CONTENTS

1

LEGACY

'This life is a test. Only a test. Had it been an actual life, you would have received further instructions on where to go and what to do.' Someone Smart

SHORTLY AFTER MY GRANDMOTHER DIED I went to view her grave. I happened to wander over to the 3 headstones nearby and saw they were marked 'For The Wax Family'. I didn't know they existed until then. On the right the Mother, on the left the Father and in the middle the Daughter, meaning me. This haunts me to this day.

My philosophy: who you are in the playground is exactly who you will be at the end of your life, unless something cataclysmic happens to you or you make a supreme effort to change your story. But it must be supreme. How are these parts cast? I don't know. All I know is I just showed up one day at recess, was handed a script and assigned my character. Who cast me in this role? Was it in the stars or in the DNA? Or is there some natural selection going on like in the animal kingdom? How do they recognise head of the herd? The one with the longest tusks? The buffalo with the biggest balls? Who's the natural born joker in the cow pack? Which heifer is going to make Vegas?

So many questions.

For some reason I was not part of the common herd in playground society and I do not know why I got exiled. Perhaps my parents sprayed me with weirdness dust. They clearly wore it, so maybe I picked it up. I had absolutely no chance to be one of the popular girls as they could smell I was not of their species; so I became one of the boys. I became their lackey, a 'runt/boy' who ran their dirty chores.

To trigger a memory of why I was rejected I tried to find some photos of me as a child. I noticed I had some drawbacks. Luckily my father chronicled every moment of my life in film and photographs, from potty training to summer camp – nothing was too embarrassing. Since I was an only child the spotlight was always trained on me. When I found the evidence, I saw immediately why everyone hated me.

I had front teeth that were so protrusive they were in another time zone – about an hour in front of my face. Kids thought my name was 'Roovy' since my lip flaps didn't meet. I made our dentist very rich from reining in the 'tusks'. He fitted me with a sputnik-like head brace that didn't so much bring my teeth to me but the rest of my body up to live under them. My first year in school I pretended to be a beaver. I took apart a Davy Crockett fur hat and pinned the tail on my bottom. This meant I couldn't hear the ridicule since I was far too busy sawing down trees and building dams.

My mother encouraged my unattractiveness by cutting my hair in a bowl shape, like a monk. She would also dress me in outfits to ensure I'd look older than her and uglier. Long before *The Sound of Music* I was in full dirndl and lederhosen. From four years old on, I was dressed as an Alpinian sheep-herder while my mother was decked out in Yves Saint Laurent, Oscar de la Renta and Valentino couture.

You could hear an intake of breath as people realised such a bombshell had released something as plain as me. She always wore a mink coat or fox fur wrap where the head ate its own tail, smoking non-stop those extra long cigarettes. She was the beauty in the house, I didn't have a chance, I could only ever be understudy waiting for her demise. There she was, this golden goddess, nyloned legs soaring up from Italian, La Dolce Vita, high heels with leather ankle straps. I yearned for those legs and shoes; instead my feet were encased in saddle shoes, which she said I needed so I wouldn't develop bunions. (I did anyway to spite her. Ha ha.) On shopping expeditions I'd scream for black patent leather pumps but they might have made me attractive so I never got them. Just hush puppies to keep me hushed. And I'd get, 'Come on Ruby, they're cute, believe me I'm your mother I would tell you.' Sometimes, I'd sneak into her closet, which was off-limits, and see rows and rows of designer shoes lined up as if for an SS inspection.

Even as an infant things were strange. I know here in England, as children, you were read stories about Pooh Bear and his tiggily-wiggily friends. I was read German stories about Strange Peter who had twelve-inch nails and frizzed up hair like he had just been electrocuted. He would set fire to people for fun or cut off their thumbs for a laugh. Grimm's Fairy Tales was another bedtime favourite. I remember one charming character, Frau Rotzkauph (translation: snot-head) had a beard, a wart and ate her children. Then she proceeded to cook them in a pie for not washing their hands before eating. There was another tale about a goose that ate a whole family and how they had to be cut out of its carcass with an axe. They all jumped out smiling but covered in bile. I didn't need night-mares, they were read to me. It all makes perfect sense when

you think that young Hitler must have gone to beddy-byes
hearing those same enchanting little tales.

Even without this bedtime reading, I was somewhat nihilis-
tic. I knew as an infant, when you lost your tooth, you were
supposed to picture a beautiful fairy with wings and a wand
who flew into your bedroom in the night to bring money just
for you. By about five, I knew this was for a 'limited season'
only and that later on I could have whole root canals and
there'd be nothing under my pillow. And when I got older, it
was clear that even if I had large vital organs removed she'd be
a no-shower. I didn't believe in the tooth fairy, Santa, the
Messiah, and certainly not Mr Wonderful; I knew nobody
could save me.

Things were off-whack anyway, since I came from a
German-speaking household, which caused me great embar-
rassment. You ordered food off the menu, it sounded like you
were declaring war in Europe: 'I'll have the schvenkackten-
zinka schvinetang Ga retchkavkch...' People came out of the
kitchen with their hands up.

In German even a phrase like 'Have a nice day', 'Aren't the
butterflies lovely?' was made by bringing up a large quantity of
phlegm and spitting it in the face of the person you were
addressing. To communicate, you literally had to lash someone
to death with your tongue. My first language was German,
which was so helpful at my nursery school called Busy Beaver.

It was cruel to send me so ill-equipped, not speaking the language of the nation I happened to be a citizen of ... but it was only the beginning.

To try and understand my parents, I'd like to give you a little history. It won't last long because they never told me much.

They escaped from Austria in 1938 though they never discussed the specifics of their departure. It was only recently that I found my mother's passport, complete with red J for Jew, and the stamp of the swastika. My mother indicated that she had practically waltzed out of Vienna, being a great beauty of the age. I recently found a suitcase full of letters, pleading to my parents (then safe in America) to get papers for the writer to help his family escape. These were followed by other letters saying their young cousin Max was now in a camp. My parents never mentioned there were family members exterminated in the camps, let alone the fact that his name was Max which is the name of my son. Finally, four years ago, at a Deli called 'Barnum and Bagel', when I asked again if I had any relatives in Austria, my mother casually replied, 'Oh, yes, they were burned', and continued eating her muffin.

Everyone who remembers her would always tell me how beautiful she was, the perfect Aryan. She had blonde hair, turquoise eyes, a figure 8 body – just the way the Nazis liked their master race. When she was a toddler, my father used to babysit for her. After many years of a disintegrating marriage he told me he regretted that he hadn't held a pillow over her face when he had the chance. But back then, she developed into a glorious creature and he pursued and won her. It must be odd, changing a girl's pants one minute and a few years later trying to get into them.

They were married the last day Jews could legally get married in Nazi Germany, joining a queue with one hundred other couples. The rabbi literally ran down the line, shouting, 'I now pronounce you man and wife.' After the wedding my father went straight to jail. The law was you had to serve time for being a Jew. The bad news was, when you got out you were still one, so you had to go back in again. He was put in a labour camp, but in his telling it sounded fun. Each prisoner had to teach a class to the other inmates. My father ran daily aerobics. Afternoons were spent digging ditches, but a particular Nazi stood in front of him so he could stretch his back without being noticed – it all seemed like a great adventure. This particular Nazi, who was probably in love with my mother, sneaked correspondence between my parents, which was written in code. In these postcards, each weather condition represented a different financial transaction, so my father could carry on his business. The Jews weren't supposed to do business, which is like telling a fish to stay away from liquids. That Nazi was eventually caught and shot for being my parents' go-between.

My mother got out early because she was sponsored by our Chicago relatives, the Hambourgers, to whom she was related on her mother Julia's side. When she got on the train, three Nazis stood up to let her lie down across the seat. They never got around to checking the passport. If you're beautiful, the rules can be broken. Later in life, she treated these relatives (who saved her life) appallingly. She used to whoop at them like they were American Indians or address them as if they were savages who spoke 'with forked tongue'. Because of course she came from such a high culture and they were down there in the primordial slime with their donuts and baseball bats. Hers was a kind of Blanche Dubois reality, where she was queen and those around her were there to serve.

My father wasn't so lucky on his exit from Austria. His family was warned when he escaped from jail, if they found him, he'd be shot on sight. He tried to escape into Switzerland by skiing over the border from Germany. Unfortunately, thousands of other Jews had the same idea and the mountain was so packed, no one could move. It was probably the last time so many Jews were on the slopes. The non-skiers didn't make it. They were herded up and sent back to Austria, from where my father tried desperately to emigrate to Australia, Africa, Holland, England, Belgium: the policy was always the same: 'No more Jews', their quotas were 'filled'. Finally, he sneaked onto a cruise ship bound for the World's Fair, in New York

City. He pretended to be an American, but the only image of one he had was James Cagney from the movies. So he got himself a gangster-type hat and spoke German with that tough guy, Yankee-sounding twang. The moment his feet hit America, he was practically U-turned back to the Fatherland. But because my mother pleaded with the authorities, he was allowed to stay. Probably, a decision she regretted throughout her life.

They lived in poverty in Chicago, but they swore they'd be rich some day. My father, driven by that immigrant spirit, with a sausage in one hand and the determination of a Rottweiler to sell it, became a success story. He told me he would walk across Chicago in pursuit of a sale. If he made a nickel, he'd save it, eating one slice of bread to give him strength for the journey home. My mother worked in a lingerie shop under the subway tracks; they shared a tiny apartment with furniture borrowed from the relatives. They saved and saved and never spent money, then slowly one sausage became two and two became an empire.

My father was ruthless. The Edward Wax Casing Company was the last remaining casing company in Chicago by the time he sold it – twice. Do you know what casings are? The piece of skin around the sausage that gives it that appetising shape – it's made out of the intestines of pigs, sheep and cows. He was always an expert in taking out your insides. The whole process of making casings is sort of like putting the farmyard in a blender and shoving it into a condom. I was always ashamed about his career so I told people he was a fashion designer for hot dogs. In Chicago, in those days, the industry was Mafia run, so you might wonder how he survived, while others went under. His vice-president, Robert – a black American – told me that no-one used revenge better than my father. Once he put someone on the shit list he spent his life hunting them down, just like The Terminator, only he was smiling. I always imagined that scene in *The Godfather*, where some guy wakes up with a horse head next to him, was probably my dad's idea of a get-well greeting card. He was tough and took no prisoners – including his wife and daughter.

I remember him shouting lovingly to his secretary, an obese loudmouth in a wig, 'Hey Barbara, how many abortions have you had today?' And she'd lovingly shout back: 'Fuck you Eddie.' God, they had fun. And so did his factory workers who stood up to their rubber boot tops in entrails-infused water, checking for holes in miles of pig intestines. Who wouldn't want to do that? Throughout my life my father would drag me to his factory and proudly say: 'Some day this will all be yours.' After I grew up, he used to pressure me to find a husband who could take over his empire when he died. I'd point out that telling a guy I was the heiress of a factory filled with pig guts didn't seem the most tantalising pick-up line.

Oh yes, I remember those visits. My father would shout to everyone at their pig intestine blowing stations, 'Here's Ruby, she's back from Europe,' like they should all pop the champagne to celebrate my arrival. Instead, they'd give me a look that said, 'Die in hell, bitch.' My father in his infinite insensitivity would go on about how they'd all been discussing me, how much they missed me, how eager they'd been for news. I have more than a few group shots of the workers, up to their knees in pig intestine juice, glaring at me like they want to stick a knife in my heart. (Very reminiscent of that scene where Caesar and Brutus and the gang are all together for the last time.)

Family-wise, we three should not have been in a house together. The air was toxic with revenge and fury. My parents used me like a round of ammo ricocheting between them. Of course, they loved me too and in the name of love wanted the best for me, which was the best for them. Things were fine and normal when I was a tiny blank blob of baby fat; a little something they could project their hopes onto. Then they realised this doll had a mouth and out of it came opinions different to theirs. I was cute till I spoke, but unlike our dog, I could not be trained. So war was declared and the biggest casualties occurred during mealtimes.

I tolerated this treatment from a young age because my father constantly told me he was leaving me a fortune. He never gave exact numbers but made a noise in his throat that indicated it was vast. He always told me I'd never need to work; now I know this was to ensure my dependency on him. His constant reminders of my stupidity were unconsciously intended to cripple me. On visits back home when I was older, our weekly ritual was to go to the bank, down to the safety deposit vaults, where I'd have to stand outside to wait for him. Inside I could hear him opening his box and rattling papers. He'd shout back through the door, 'Boy, Ruby have you got a lot of money. I wish someone left me a fortune like this.' As a child, whenever he'd beat me, I'd mentally charge him for it. I kept an account book of the humiliations in my head. By my calculations by the time I was grown, he owed me ten million dollars. When I finally inherited, the actual numbers were waaaaay off.

You can imagine by the time I hit puberty, in the 1960s, how angry they must have been. How resentful that I was lucky enough to be a teenager during this time of full sexual liberation, when America was having an orgy, while their youth had been fixated on how to flee death. So when at 16 I started to think about the opposite sex, the prison walls came rattling down, the drawbridge was hauled up, the windows bolted and locked. They kept me confined to my room, insisting it was for my own good but it was more for theirs. At the front door, friends could hear the battle cries. But I was as tenacious as they were and I escaped out the bedroom window – recreating time and again their escape from Austria. It was, in a small way, an homage. Later, I would literally escape to another country to get away from them. They fled Europe, I fled back again.

And so when I began chasing (no, stalking) a musician from the cast of *Hair*, my family hit meltdown. I would return from a night of … well, really no sex at all. I was so petrified of the act, I would lie on the musician's bed, legs bolted shut and lips pressed together to prevent any form of entry. He'd poke and prod but the only way he could possibly have penetrated me was if he had a buzz saw strapped on. Let's just say he lost interest – fast. But my parents would wait up for me, shouting that I was a slut (in my dreams). I wasn't given a key to the door so I'd have to ring the bell, my mother would rip it off its hinges, screeching, 'Run, run with the hyenas! I'm living with a mother-murderer and sadist like her father. If you go to bed with dogs you wake up with fleas.'

And so this pattern continued; each night I'd escape, lie in this boy's bed, solid as ice, then drive home and be inspected by both parents for signs of sex or drugs. My father would empty the contents of the car ashtray and make me identify what was what. Gum wrapper, cigarette butt, roach … if he found a roach he'd shout, 'Yavana-mary.' (Not being able to pronounce marijuana.) Before he could smack me, I'd have escaped upstairs and locked myself in the bathroom.

This nightly inspection and beating continued until the damage was truly done. I froze. I literally froze, both emotionally and sexually. But I kept going to see this hippie boy out of spite. I was being trained to connect sex with spite, certainly not love – that was in the freezer both for my parents and for anyone else for a long time. So I learned to enjoy the deceit because clearly there was no real pleasure in the act.

My relationship with my parents gnawed away at much of my life, until three years ago when my father had a stroke. When he lost control of his power I became liberated. It's that simple. And the more he lost control, the less crippled I became and the more fully human. My father used to speak about eight languages but each day after the stroke, his mind unravelled a little more. One by one, the languages would be erased in the order of his learning them: one day Spanish – gone, next Italian – gone, then Portuguese – gone, until he could only remember his native German. Even then it was only fragments, incomplete sentences, wherein he seemed to be trying to remember why he had been so angry at me. I'd hear the beginning of a punishment and then a fade out, 'Boy are you in trouble … you forgot to … that's typical Ruby …' Then nothing. The tape of his memory was pulled from his mind that quickly. And when his rage went, so did my mother's, it just seeped away, leaving her with the charm she had probably had as a child, a long time ago, before I met her.

What made everyone so mad? What was all the commotion about? All that energy wasted on all that anger when we could have been friends. Both are in a home now and neither can remember – so why should I? But the more they lost power, the more I opened and thawed. And so at this very late age, the war was over.

2

YOUTH

'Once upon a time ...' Einstein

I GREW UP IN EVANSTON, Illinois, which looks like an ad for the American Dream: leafy streets are bridged by giant oak trees and feature brightly painted Victorian houses surrounded by wraparound porches, each residence showing off more elaborate latticework than the one before, as if saying, 'Up yours, get this!' to the next.

I attended the nearby Lincoln School. Recess was a time to cull the weak from the strong. I still wince from the pain of being kicked off the seesaw to make room for a cooler girl. I remember the femme fatale, Jody Kindsley. She had breasts at age four, which she stuck out like trophies, and golden locks that she would hand-flick like a professional shampoo girl in the TV ads. When she'd go down the slide, it was a thing of beauty and grace. All the boys were in love and would throw her in the pool while she screamed in protest. I would stand poolside and scream. 'Don't throw me in.' And they never did.

One of my jobs as runt/boy was to accost girls. I would move stealthily towards the playground, with camouflage smeared across my face where a girl called Carol was always hanging upside down on the jungle gym. The daily ritual was that I would pull down her underpants (or up because she was hanging upside down) and because I knew where they were, put chipboard pieces into her private parts. It was dirty work but someone had to do it, and since it was my job, I did it well.

Our house was situated on a lake, across the street from a park – a classical white, square Victorian house with dark green shutters. My mother had the top floor removed so she could cut down on dusting; I think this might be an original concept.

We had a large flower garden, dominated by a cherry tree, which was planted when I was born and later cut down when it flourished a little too much. We always picked the cherries in the summer and I remember they made me pucker with their bitterness.

Inside, the house was almost in complete darkness. My mother kept the curtains shut because she thought the sunlight was going to 'eat our furniture'. Our neighbours lived in a glass house so they could see the lake, but the sunlight wasn't interested in their house, only ours. We did have one large picture window in the living room and this is where I would sit and stare out at life in the park – watching normal people having barbeques and throwing Frisbees – always filled with yearning to be part of their family. I fantasised about getting into their car and going home to live with them. Even when I'd venture out and walk among them I'd still feel like I was in a bubble that kept me separate. My dog Lumpi sat beside me staring out of the window, his wet nose squashed up to the glass – he wanted out too.

Downstairs, the house featured white walls splattered with gold, black and silver paint. I remember how my mother walked into the living and dining area, paint buckets strapped around her waist and flicking with her hands, splattering paint on the walls. The effect was like the scene of a murder – like someone's insides were filled with paint before being viciously bludgeoned to death.

Chipped ashtrays and broken vases were left over from some of our more operatic fights. Above the black fireplace, there was a fresco of life-sized Roman soldiers; they too were splattered in silver and gold. I wouldn't bring friends home because everything was covered in plastic and I was ashamed; the sofas, the lamps, wall hangings, even the trinkets on the tables were still in their boxes. It was like everything was gift-wrapped so dust couldn't get at them. When it was hot outside you'd get up with the sofa sticking to your backside – really whenever you got up off anything in the house there was a burping sound, not to mention the welts left on the backs of your thighs. Whenever I'd come home, I always half-expected to find my father covered in the plastic, dust-free, dead and perfectly preserved.

He was always glued, literally, in his green corner chair, listening to the opera at top volume. I don't know where it ended and my mother's screaming started. 'His Highness is a misogynist and wife torturer – always running with the animals and the perverts, he makes me vomit!' The opera blared and blended with my mother who would be ranting fortissimo, 'I should bow to Mr Wax, who crawled from the sewers of Galicia with his mother, the insane cripple.' Then she would shine her beam on me. 'And you Ruby, are as poisoned as him. You, a Mother murderer, running with the shmoes and the schlemiels – the lowlifes … They mean everything to you and not your mother.' She'd then sink to her knees and hold out a pair of scissors. 'Cut my heart out, with a scissor!' And then apropos of nothing she'd scream, 'Toscanini!' on the top of her lungs – that was the scary bit.

At the end of her aria, my father would slam his hand down on the radio and yell, 'Shut up now Berta, we've had enough hysteria; Ruby, don't listen to her or you'll end up neurotic like your mother.' She'd continue howling and then he'd drag her upstairs to their bedroom and behind the door I'd hear him belt her. I once walked into their room when he was striking her, she on the floor, he straddling her. They both looked up dripping with sweat and said, 'Mommy and daddy are playing ha ha we're having fun! Close the door!' and I did. As I walked away the belting started up again.

My room was next door to theirs. It was filled with girly furniture, frilly lampshades and two child-sized beds. It had white drawers with blue trim and a matching dressing table filled with my secret diaries and tokens. Knowing that my mother constantly trawled through my things, I buried most of my private treasures in the garden – in a hole.

On my girly dressing table was a music box ringed with Mother Goose figures that went in a merry-go-round circle as the music played. Even at seven I saw it as a symbol of a broken childhood. Whenever we'd fight I'd throw the music box at their bedroom door in frustration, the figurines cracked off in the flinging and so only certain limbs remained, circling to the eerie music. All that was left was Little Red Riding Hood's arm or Pinocchio's left leg. My mother would attempt to glue the broken bits back on but then another fight would ignite and Goldilocks' head would come off.

My mother would never let me make my own bed because it had to be perfect, not with lumps and creases. I tried a few times, shaking under her watchful eye. When I finished she'd scream like a banshee, 'Look, look at the wrinkles! You're blind, deaf and a moron torturer like your Father' and she'd crawl on the floor shrieking for me to 'watch and learn' as she pulled, with her teeth, bed sheet and blanket to perfect angles tucking them in taut, to tearing point. Painstakingly, she'd cover the whole thing with the blue and white swirly bedspread, 'I vant it parallel to the bed corners. Parallel!' It would take hours as she sweated and growled gutturally while making the perfect bed.

Order and cleanliness were her reasons for living; all my clothes would be folded and put in plastic bags. My underwear had razor-edged seams down both sides. Each night my mother waited outside the bathroom door and as I removed them she'd almost suck them out of my hands, run downstairs and scrub them clean. The following morning they would miraculously appear, still hot from the iron, folded like origami in the drawer. If I dared to pull my Fruit of the Loom underpants at random from the drawer, she'd enter my room like a hurricane, rip them from my hand and begin refolding them and stuffing them back in the plastic bags. This is why I always thought the film *Mommie Dearest* was a sitcom. I thought the expression 'No more wire hangers' was a normal salutation like 'Have a Nice Day.'

Down in the pits of the house was the basement. You descended stone steps into what can only be described as a replica of a German beer keller. The walls were all wood-panelled and you sat on cushioned beer barrels; when you stood up you would hit leaves since my mother laced plastic vines around the hot water pipes, which veined the ceiling. To keep with the 'Keller' theme we had a cuckoo clock on the wall. The clock had been hurled once too often during a family fight so the bird, despite being broken with its head hanging off and its beak missing, managed to croak at you on the hour.

My strongest memory is of a carved, wooden miniature German bar, on which men, sitting on barrels, drank from tankards. The men were grotesques with warts, bulbous noses and blotchy faces. When you pulled off a head, you found that the rest of the body was a corkscrew. If you pulled off another, his body was a bottle opener – it was the stuff which night-mares are made of – and I had many. My most frequent recur-ring nightmare was set in a Swiss village where a half-wolf, half-man had been eating children's genitals. The victims were instantly recognisable; they walked with glazed eyes and legs apart. I went to find the wolf's house and looked in his window where I saw smoked babies hanging from the ceiling like carcasses in a butcher store. Clearly my unconsciousness was on overdrive.

But the scariest room was the kitchen. It looked like the normal, clean wooden-shelved kitchen of sitcoms; it even had the breakfast nook consisting of a yellow horseshoe-shaped plastic banquette surrounding a Formica table – but it was at this kitchen table that war took place, nightly. Each dinnertime we had hot dogs because of my father's large stash of them back at the sausage factory and since my mother wouldn't use the oven, in order to avoid stains, it made perfect sense to her to boil the dogs every night. I begged for something else so my mother once put toothpicks in the sides of the hot dogs to make wings and said they were chickens. Once she did boil a chicken in a pot and I lived to regret it, from out of the top rim came a naked yellow claw as if it was trying to escape. It wasn't dissimilar to my grandmother's hand and for a moment I thought she was boiled.

I loved my grandmother, whom I called Omi. She was 89 years old so her mind was a little fried. While Mommy wiped the kitchen, Omi would sneak me candy under the table. Her mission in life was to save the little girl from the evil mother. At night, I'd sneak into her bed and snuggle into her huge breasts, my father would have to come and drag me out by the ankles. He pulled his back out once and had to wear a girdle for the rest of his life, ha ha. Omi would follow my mother around the house, sprinkling crumbs on the floor while my mother leapt like a person whose feet were on fire to absorb them. She knew how to make my mother crazy – I come from a long line of spite. When my mother would chase me out of the house screaming at me for not washing the dishes, Omi would be behind, snatching her hair to pull her off me. Then they'd go at each other like two cartoon characters, fighting each other in a ball of fury.

Once a day my Grandmother Omi would make an appearance from the attic wearing those large, pink, old person underpants around her ankles; she wore those lilac, flowered, old lady dresses and smelled of cabbage, formaldehyde and face powder. If she really liked you she would cram a pair of her false teeth into your hand. Which is nice. It was like handing you a smile. Some days she'd put the teeth in wrong, she'd put the upper teeth on her lower gums and the lower teeth on her upper gums. She'd look like she was trying to eat her own head. On certain days I'd find her in the empty bathtub completely naked. I'd ask her what she was doing and she'd say, 'Fishing.' When the front doorbell rang, she'd answer the fridge and I'd say, 'Who was it, Omi?' And she'd answer, 'Head of lettuce, no message.'

As we ate meals together, I'd hear the water running from the faucet and my skin would crawl. To this day I can't stomach that sound because it reminds me of her rinsing out that

sponge just before she'd come over and do a 'big wipe'. My
mother would sit across from me, like a recoiled cheetah waiting for a crumb to drop from my lips. When it did she'd fly
across the room in vulture position, sweep that sponge across
my face, down across the plate, through the food, along the
table leg, across the floor, through the dog stuff, out the door,
down the sidewalk and onward unless she was restrained. I
never saw her without a sponge. This is a woman who spent
her life hunched over with a sponge in each hand. She'd walk
around bent over because she'd insist we open doors from the
bottom – this would prevent us getting finger marks on the
door knobs. I bought her a black sponge on Mother's Day, for
formal wear.

She had two distinct personalities: one personality was so
adorable that people would say, 'Your mother is so sweet, why
are you being so mean about her?' She'd smile at my friends.
'Oh you're Ruby's little friends. That's charming.' Then she'd
turn her head to me, assume personality number two and
scream, 'Another bum from the slums of Chicago, I could
vomit!' and that was in her good mood. In personality number
two, she could swing to the Outer Hebrides of madness.
Another example: she'd be in mid-conversation while watching
TV. 'You know, I like that show *Dallas*, it's a sophisticated soap
opera.' Then suddenly, werewolf transformation and she'd
shriek 'I vant the carpet parallel to the vall! Make it parallel!'

She'd fly to the floor and make the carpet parallel, clawing at the rug. Everything in the house had to be parallel. My grandmother once fell down the stairs – my mother ran over and made her parallel to the wall. I escaped at right angles.

Sitting on the stool at the breakfast nook was my saviour, our cleaning woman Gheta. Although she wore a maid's uniform and always called my mother Mrs Wax, secretly she was my mother's best friend. She never lifted a finger for as long as I can remember because she had my mother sussed. She'd go, 'Ms Wax show me how to wash tem dishes again?' My mother would jump to the dishes demonstrating, 'You vipe it in a clockwise position. It's clockwise.' Then Gheta would move onto the floor and say, 'Remind me Ms Wax how do you do the floor, I forgot?' My mother would hit the floor going, 'Into the corners, push, push, push.' Gheta just watched with a cigarette dangling out of her mouth thinking, 'That honky sucker.' But I liked Gheta, she was my ally and she'd tip me off when my mother was on the rampage. Gheta would say, 'Your mama's coming and she be really crazy today, run for your life.'

On the floor was Lumpi, jumping up to get at the food on the table. Omi offered him crusts of bread and cookies in a closed fist so Lumpi humped her arm constantly, thinking he was giving her pleasure in exchange for those crusts. My grandmother wore him like cuff links, like he was a canine accessory and this is while you're trying to eat. Actually he humped everyone all the time because my parents denied him sex. I knew how he felt. So when he'd glue himself onto someone's leg and cha cha, my mother would scream with delight, 'Oh, look. The lover boy is dancing. He's dancing.' Guests would try to smile at his antics while graciously wiping him off their leg. I once tried to fix him up in the park with a female but he was so used to humping leg, he rejected the real thing.

His other party piece was to lift his paw straight out as my mother shrieked, 'Lumpi say Heil Hitler.' The room would be silenced. She loved that dog to unnatural proportions; she sang songs to him for every occasion – all in German and at a volume that could shatter your eardrums: an ambulance siren could be drowned out when she let it rip. There was a song for Lumpi's 'walkies' and a song for Lumpi's 'eaties'. I will give you the songs so you can sing along (to be sung to the tune of the William Tell Overture); the lyrics in German, literally translated, mean: 'The dog goes for a walk. The dog goes for a walk. For a walk, goes the dog.' (It's better in German.) The eating song is the same tune but the lyrics are: 'The dogs is going to eat, the dog is going to eat. Eat is the dog going to do.'

You get the idea.

When the first Lumpi died at age 147 in dog years, my mother went around the country to find a replica with a photo of the dead Lumpi. She drove from kennel to kennel, state to state, searching for his identical markings, but she neglected to tell me the news of his death. So when I came back from college, there was a tiny version of the senile one, leaping up in the air. When I had left you had to drag him from tree to tree and hand-lift his leg for peeing, now he scampered like a puppy. When I questioned the situation, my mother just said, 'Lumpi's soul had been passed,' like the Dalai Lama of the fox terrier world. You can imagine how alarmed I was when my grandmother died. I was scared I'd find a nubile, body-double in the house after the funeral.

When I think back on that breakfast nook, I could just choke with the frustration I felt – how they were all talking at someone who was the fantasy of their child, not the real me. I felt I wanted to bludgeon them many, many times and then pull them apart with my bare hands, but I needed a lift to school. We were all like different planets orbiting a bowlful of hot dogs but united in anger, like the Addams Family on TV but weirder cause we weren't in costume.

When life at home got too bizarre I'd head out into the streets where my neighbour Mrs Gross would fly by. The whole neighbourhood was Austrian. I don't know if you're familiar with that temperament – nervous? Her hair was on anti-depressants, I mean wired. She'd be dragging her dog Trixie around behind her, leaving skidmarks on the sidewalk. This boxer was stiff, he'd been dead for about four months but she didn't know it. I'd say innocently, 'How's it goin', Mrs Gross?' And she'd go, using her arms like crazy hedge clippers, 'I should eat Polish sausages, how should I know? I'm living in a country full of mental defectives; we might as well be living in teepees, Mrs Weltzer hasn't picked up a leaf for ten years.' (She spoke like my mother.) Then she'd rev up and skid out, leaving me alone on the sidewalk looking for fellow earthlings – but back to our house.

During dinner my father worked the phone, hustling pig intestines; he clearly didn't know who he was speaking to but knew how to charm. My father started all conversations with, 'Hello blue eyes.' I always wondered how the men reacted. Sometimes he'd get his colloquialisms mixed up; he'd come up with 'Vel, dats da vey da chickens crumble.' To many customers, he was the epitome of European charm: they all said he was like Charles Boyer – he sort of was, suave and meticulously dressed in a crisp white shirt and tie or after dinner in his manly silk dressing gown. To me he was the embodiment of punishment. He tried to train me to be obedient, using the same method he tried with Lumpi, including soap in my mouth, hairbrushes, belts and locking me in my room with no food. He never got the dog to stop peeing on the floor and he never got me to behave. A few years before his stroke, he said he hadn't hit me enough and that's why I ended up so unruly. His job was to control and terrorise; that's what his father did and he wanted to pass this gift on.

When I got big enough in size, I started to fight back. Once, after some heavy abuse, I told them to 'Shut up or I'll hang myself from my handbag strap.' This wasn't easy, as 'death by purse' isn't really a *practised* art.

I remember on more than one occasion, my mother opening the passenger door and kicking me into the road while driving at 30 miles an hour. People would stop her and say they were going to report her for child abuse. She would answer, 'What are you talking about, I'm getting her to dancing class?'

She sent me to jazz dance class at age ten; she wanted to make me more like her and thought dance would sophisticate me up and give me confidence. At the Gus Giordono Dance studio all the other girls were fully developed except for me, they were teenagers. You had to dance all thrusty and jazzy, big sexy hip swings and snapping fingers like Sammy Davis Junior. 'Kick, flick, head swing, hip thrust, thrust', to wild, blaring sax and drums. I was so ashamed, I'd run to the back of the class and try and seep in a crack. My mother would open the door and scream, 'Get your finger out of your nose and dance!' She was always watching, like Big Brother. So I'd pretend to go to the bathroom and then run out onto the streets; where I was going I didn't know, it was just blind panic. She would get in her car and practically drive on the sidewalk, roll down the window and scream, 'Get in the car, Mother murderer, I'm eating my heart out,' but I kept running so she'd shout,

'Rooooooovyyyy I'm talking to you.' Jewish people came out of their homes to surrender: they thought the Gestapo was back in town.

Once, after another violent fight, I ran out of the house in my pyjamas during a snow storm. My mother ran after me in her nightgown and fell into a six foot deep hole. She shouted up at me, 'I must have got radiation in me when I was carrying you, you imbecile; otherwise you wouldn't be so rambunctious' – I had to stop myself from kicking snow in the hole and covering her up. I only stopped because I was scared I'd get caught, otherwise today she would be a popsicle. My bare feet were freezing so I climbed on a car roof and held them in the air. She finally got out of the hole still screaming at me to come home. 'I criticise you for your own good – if I don't tell you, who will? No one will ever love you like your mother.' Eventually I ran home and at the front door she greeted me with a bucket of hot water to defrost my bare, frozen feet. To this day I can't go in the cold without getting the sensation that someone is sticking a million bamboo shoots in the soles of my feet – a souvenir from childhood.

My mother didn't believe in smoking on the Sabbath, so each Saturday would begin with the spectacle of my nicotine-starved mother, wild like Beelzebub, possessed, chasing me through the house, my father chasing her and my grandmother bringing up the rear. Around one o'clock in the morning, the police would arrive complaining wearily, 'Oh, it's the Waxs again.' Usually the bravest bull cop would pry us off each other, take me aside and mumble, 'I got to explain something to youse. Youse mother's goin' through what we calls' (then he'd blush) 'the change – meno … somethin'… so like, lay off.' Which was like saying a hurricane is a gust of wind with an attitude. I was tempted to say if he was right, according to my calculations, my mother had been going through menopause for about thirty years.

Later in life when I'd return home from Europe, my parents would greet me, grinning from ear to ear. 'Happy to be here?' Happy? Even as an adult my house horrified me – when I had nightmares about it, it felt exactly the same as when I was awake.

Another saviour during childhood was a distant relative, through marriage, called Harriet Hambourger. I used to say the sun shone from her. From age 15 to 33, when it got too violent in our house I'd run away to hers because the smell and feeling of safety at her house was indescribably comforting. It was *verboten* to see Harriet. My mother kept asking what did I have to say to Harriet, that I couldn't say to my own mother? She was raging in jealousy. I used to lie and say I was going shopping, then my father would call Harriet and bark, 'Is she there?' He'd come over and throw me in the car. It felt like Harriet and I were clandestine lovers. (She was 32 years older than me.)

As a child I used to wonder why we couldn't be more like the families on TV. Why couldn't we have a home like *Ozzie and Harriet, Father Knows Best* or *The Donna Reed Show*? They all seemed normal: the TV Dad comes home from the office (my father arrived home in the Wiener Wagon); Dad on TV puts his briefcase down and kisses the TV Mom who is baking cookies (my mother was boiling hot dogs and wiping the house); Dad on TV calls for his daughter, 'Kitten? I'm home.' TV Girl plus fluffy dog run downstairs (TV Girl does not have to open kitchen door from below to avoid smudging knob; TV Dog is in non-hump mode). TV Mom says, 'Oh, and honey, I have a surprise, my mother's coming for dinner (not like Omi with pink pants dragging around on the floor like a mop).

I'll explain about the Wiener Wagon. My father, as I told you, ran a casing factory. His office was above that of another Sausage King, called Oscar Meyer. Oscar was a celebrity not only because he did his own ads on TV but because he drove the Wiener Wagon, a 30-foot hot dog, around Chicago. The ad ended with a bunch of loud, obnoxious kids singing the oh so irritating Oscar Meyer theme tune. 'Oh, I wish I was an Oscar Meyer Wiener. That is what I'd truly like to beeeeeee. 'Cos if I was an Oscar Meyer Wiener, everyone would be in love with me.' You wanted to clobber them to death. And, horror of horrors, Oscar would give my father lifts home in the Wiener Wagon.

Can you imagine, you're a child trying to make a friend and your father pulls up in the driveway in a 30-foot hot dog? Or he gives you a lift to school and you're trying to run away? Being kerb-crawled by a meat product? It's a miracle I'm not on heroin.

I did what I could to survive those tough school years. I made friends with a similar nerd-girl who had equally protruding frontal tusks. Tira had an overbite that threatened the next continent. We, sadly, formed a horse club, and this is how stupid I was: Tira (tusk-girl) was president of the club and I was the only member and the only person who paid dues – it took me five years to figure out she was screwing me. Also we had club contests for best drawing of a horse, with a cash prize (money from the dues). Her two-year-old brother couldn't hold a crayon, but he won the drawing contest year after year. I never caught on. We eventually bought a bridle, again out of my dues, and I only drew the line after she insisted on putting it on me and riding me around the house; I had some pride, only some – I did let her fit me for horseshoes. Once she developed breasts, she was out of the club. She eventually left me for a man; I never forgave her.

Every winter, I'd be yanked over to Miami, which I loathed – my father bought an apartment there when I was around eight. Every winter my parents would summon me with their gentle cry, 'Get over here or the dog gets the inheritance.' Do you know Miami? I'm not talking about the new South Beach end but the old Fontainebleau Hotel neighbourhood. There, Miami has improved upon what the Renaissance screwed up. In front of our condo we have the Venus de Milo only she's 40 feet tall and has arms – she looks like she's hailing a taxi. You want the leaning tower of Pisa? We got it, by the pool, but it's a lot cleaner, also it's not leaning.

Florida was discovered by Ponce de Leon who went there to discover the fountain of youth so today millions of old people go to Florida and just get older and older, ironic isn't it? Today the main sport there is eating. People sit around the pool going, 'What'ya eat? Big portions? Was it hot? Was it cold? Was it good? Did you get a fork or did you just shovel it into your mouth?' And then they will sink to the bottom of the pool and about an hour later a bubble will rise to the surface followed by them. No matter where you are in the pool they will swim straight over you, and they're still gabbling, 'How was the meat? Did it have buffalo horns and just gallop into your mouth?'

I've noticed no matter how hard the rest of the world tries, no one can glut out like an American, you can find lost relatives in those stomach rolls. The streets are lined with restaurants: 'Jonathan Livingston Seafood', 'The Cookie Crematorium', 'Tits 'N' Tacos' – all you have to do is open your mouth and run. Once you're inside it's 'All you can eat for $5.99'. People come in with a colostomy bag. When they've filled up their own stomachs, they can just plug in an extension.

The real reason I hated Miami is because my parents never really let me out of their sight. I was dragged there from age 8 to 35 and when I was a teenager and up they certainly never let me go out with a man – my father feared everyone was a potential murderer. He wouldn't even loan me the car: 'They drag you from the wheel and beat you to death.'

For the first 12 years my mother made me wear a blue terry cloth robe she got free at the bank. 'It looks cute, believe me, I'm your mother I would tell you' – I looked like a bag person in it. Then my father would command, 'Go to the beach and make friends Ruby, make friends.' (He didn't mean men.) I tried to tell him I had nothing in common with these Jewish Princesses, they have those flat tan stomachs, framed by a tiny bikini – a piece of dental floss and a nicotine patch. My father kindly pointed out I was jealous. Duh?

3

PUBERTY

'My God Miss Wax, you're beautiful ...' Shakespeare

THINGS GOT WORSE WHEN I HIT PUBERTY. I had no Donna Reed to sit on my bed and gently explain what to expect, no one was giving me any information. The moment it struck, I went into shock. It's like my organs were just sitting around chewing gum, shooting the breeze and suddenly: Bam! A big oestrogen rush and my hormones started bubbling like Vesuvius about to blow. It happened so suddenly, one day you're happy to be a horse, galloping around: 'Whoa boy.'

(Making neighing and whinnying sounds. You know you're still a kid when you don't question why the sound of the horse you're riding on is coming out of your mouth.) Then puberty hits and suddenly you're necking with your pillow, 'Oh, Rock don't be so fresh.' 'Oh, Rock you've got to behave!' I named my pillow after Rock Hudson; can you imagine the shock I went into when I found out my pillow was a homosexual? Anyway you hit puberty and you're yearning, you're yearning – you're watching TV and suddenly you want Lassie ... but you want him as a MAN.

I did my own experimentation with Barbie and Ken. I knew something about how penetration occurred but what went into what I had no idea. So I tore Barbie's head off and shoved Ken's leg in the neckhole but it didn't seem right. (Why didn't they give Ken some kind of penis? It would have cleared up so much – I guess because it's a tiny part and small children might have choked on it.)

Finally my mother figured that special time had arrived for her to explain womanhood sensitively to her young daughter. So she took me to the gorilla house at the zoo. When I asked what we were doing there, she manically pointed to Gomez and said, 'That's what happens when you grow up.'

I said 'What, I swing on a tyre?'.

Well, then I waved at him, he waved at me and then it happened – he got excited, pulled out some bludgeon-looking thing and I started screaming, 'What is that thing he's waving at me? What is that thing?'

My mother just lowered her eyes and said, 'If you ever see one of those later in life, call the police.'

I finally figured out what went in where, on a family trip to Jamaica when I saw people having sex in real life. I didn't just run into them on the side of the road or on the beach, I happened to be hanging by my toenails from the balcony to observe and report to my friends what was going on next door. When I got home I tried to replicate what I saw with my turtles, Alvin and Fran. I wanted it to be proper so I insisted they date first – after two weeks they were still just going out for burgers in their toy car. Finally I was bored, so I thought it was time they should go 'all the way', I did their voices for them: 'Oh, no Alvin I mustn't.' 'Come on Fran, we're going to get married and we love each other, let's just do it.' At this point I hit a blank so I scotch-taped them together for the night. The next day they were dead; found locked in each other's claws, stuffed with burger. Don't tell anyone, I could get taken away. I said it was date rape.

My own first sexual encounter was another experience from Planet Weird. I was about 12 years old and playing in the street with Barbie Garside; I played Rock Hudson, the faithful chauffeur, and I was peddling my employer Liz Taylor in a kind of golf cart with a fancy, fringed canopy down the road.

(I always played the male role – don't ask me why.) Barbie was in her fake mink stole wrapped around her shoulders and I wore the cap of the servant. Suddenly, some guy on the street stopped us. He said, 'Do you want to see my underwear?' It seemed to me like a good deal for Liz who was always husband-hunting. So, I said, 'Sure.' No underwear was forthcoming; instead he pulled out the full penis.

I went into shock not knowing what it was. But Barbie did, she jumped out of the cart and ran home screaming. I stayed with my vehicle because I was a professional and peddled it home at about 200 mph. My feet were circling so fast I practically burned rubber into the driveway.

My mother took her own advice on sexual matters, and immediately called the police. When the police interviewed us I was so traumatised that my imagination was running riot. I described the penis as a five foot long, purple weapon-like looking thing. The policeman cautioned, 'Ok, what youse got here, is the said male Caucasian "exposed" himself to you. Don't youse tell anyone at your school.'

At school the next day I followed his advice, I told everyone that something bad had happened to me but I wasn't supposed to say what it was. The whole school begged me to tell them, so finally, out of pity, I sold them the letters of the word 'exposed'. If you bought the whole set you could maybe piece it together – fifty cents for the 'E', a dollar for the 'X'.

That was my first experience in mixing sex with capitalism.

I spent the rest of high school learning to manipulate people because I needed an army of people who were devoted to me, to protect me from my foe – my parents. And the foe was formidable, I would need to enlist such a large number of allies that it seemed everyone in my hometown would have to become my friend. I joined – not really joined – latched onto a gang called the Vandelous Virgins. We were tough, we were cool and we spray painted 'VV' on every opportune surface in town. Sometimes if a person was particularly creepy we spray-painted them. I had a job (bottom peg) which was to gain the confidence of the creepy person and lure them out of the school, telling them the coast was clear. As soon as the creepy person ventured out in the open I gave the signal and the VVs would thunder past me, weapons ready, and spray the said victim in paint.

A few years ago, in London, I was recognised by a victim of the VVs. Why was she a target at the time? Because she was a nerd and fat – cardinal sins at age 12. She was perhaps one rung below me on the popularity scale, so it was a relief to be victimising her (see food chain). Anyway, she reminded me that after I lured her out of school, this group of hoodlums had filled her handbag with ketchup and sprayed her green. What could I say? 'Sorry. Better you than me.' I tried to explain about it being a dog eat dog world and that I was just doing my job but she just turned her back on me, still traumatised.

After the stint as gang member, I started to build my own army with, well really anyone who liked me. I needed large numbers so I became a serial 'befriender'. First I focused on the splinter groups – the weirdos, the pre-hippies, the 'nearly nerdy'. Once I had been assured of their love, I moved to the next rung on the social ladder. One day, in a stroke of genius, I paid 25 cents to the most popular girl at school to come to my house. When I told everyone she was coming, the response was exactly what I'd hoped for, everyone agreed: 'Oh, if Cindy likes her, then we like her.' I was probably using tactics familiar to Pamela Harriman and other killer socialites. The thicker my address book, the safer I felt. I had an insatiable appetite to conquer all before me. So, as the expression goes, I worked the room all through high school.

I only took time off when my parents sent me to summer camp. I first started going when I was eight and when my mother first told me I'd be leaving home for two months, I cried. Why? Children will always cling to what's familiar even if it's the source of their pain.

When my mother said she'd pick me up, a light bulb came on and I not only stayed but insisted on going to camp for the next eight years – this thing called camp was the greatest gift they ever gave me.

At Camp Agawak, which probably means 'kiss my ass' in Red Indian, they taught everything a young girl should know

– tossing a javelin, working in leather goods and how to load a rifle. This camp, no matter how weedy you were, would make a man out of you. It was set in the North Woods of Wisconsin – a dense forest of birch trees, dotted with log cabins, teepees and totem poles, surrounding a crystal blue, canoe-crammed lake. The campers were divided into two teams, Blue and White; I was a devoted Blue for nine years. To this day nothing – I mean nothing – has ever meant as much as being a Blue. Not the outcome of the Vietnam War, not the downfall of the Taliban, not Saddam Hussein, nothing.

We'd sing war chants like, 'Give a yell, give a yell, give a good substantial yell. And when we yell we yell like this and this is what we yell. L and M. L and M. L and M Diego, San Diego. Ishki Pishki, kick him in the kiski. Hockus pockus try and choke us, yeah, Blues!' Then you'd build yourself into a frenzy and go in there and play miniature golf. We were told if we were losing we shouldn't be afraid to use a handgun. (I'm joking.) Every morning you had to line up in order of your father's income. (I'm joking again. But it was important.) From morning till night we competed not just Blues against Whites but against each other, each cabin, each age, each hair colour, the opportunities for competition were never-ending.

The bugle blew at 06:00. The girls would leap from bed and run to line up for flag raising. Our heels would have to form a straight line; the older girls were 'spotters' and would shout, 'Back a little! Left foot forward! Stop!' until we achieved precision. Then Helen, the Major General, made her inspection, as we stood rigidly to attention. Sometimes as Helen contemplated heel lines a young girl might faint from the pressure and from standing stiffly for half an hour. Her fellow team members would try and hold her upright, but once Helen announced the winner we were 'at ease' and would drop her on her head. Then off we'd scamper to the next competition – who had the cleanest nails.

The rest of the day was war. There were competitions on the lake for canoeing, using paddles to beat the other team back from the finish line, archery competitions where the target was the other team, solo challenges for personal points in tennis, horse riding, gunmanship, ping-pong, swimming, water-skiing, arts and crafts, singing, trampoline, pole-vaulting etc.

My first crush was on the water-ski coach whose name was Beaver. I am not making that up – everybody loved her, she was so strong and handsome and clearly a dyke. We'd sing to her, 'We love you Beaver oh yes we do. We love you Beaver and we'll be true. When you're not with us, we're blue. Oh, Beaver we love you.' When Beaver would reluctantly in her shy, mannish way, hand out awards in water-skiing, we took it as a sign of love. At age eleven, I was going over twelve foot ski jumps, backwards. I did not do this for the love of skiing – I did it for Beaver. That's how crazy in love I was. It didn't go anywhere.

At the end of the first month we looked forward with excitement to parents' weekend; the problem was all the parents looked the same, it could take the whole weekend to figure out which ones were yours. From out of identical Cadillacs, identical Jewish mothers emerged – so over-tanned they could pass as handbags, crocodile smiles with neon pink lips, usually bleeding onto the teeth. They looked like very old, exhausted elephants in stretch pants, some faces were lifted so high it was like trying to hold up soup with scaffolding. Their voices reminded me of hoarse, croaky wild ducks, as they'd honk orders at the husband. 'Sheldon get me a chair. Leo pull up your pants!' The husbands wore identical golf slacks and looked shell-shocked. There was a look in their eyes that said, 'No more, I give up.'

My parents once showed up a day late for parents' weekend when I was 13. I spotted their Cadillac coming down the driveway with a dead, mutilated deer smeared on the front bumper – a hoof here, an antler splayed there, some part of an organ and an eye on the windshield. My parents opened their car door smiling in triumph; I wondered how far off the road they had to drive to slaughter their prey.

Another year they sprung another surprise. My father was with me the whole day, which was spent in competition. He cheered as I blew a ping-pong ball over a football field, all the other parents were down on all fours, screaming, 'Come on baby, blow that ball.' Later that night my father said he had a surprise for me, took me to the car, opened the trunk and my mother climbed out. There are some things I will never understand.

The most gruelling battle was 'Capture the Flag' – an event that took three days. We wore camouflage and face-paint and when a bell rang the Blue and White Defence and Offence teams spread out fast to cover the three-mile war zone. To capture the other team's flag, the Offence would scuba dive in the lake, ride horses and practically parachute into the enemy terrain. If caught by the enemy, you were held in jails unless one of your team rescued you. Some people were tortured a little. My last year when I was the captain, I said, 'There will be no girls on defence this year. When Helen rings the bell, we'll all run as a cluster bomb towards the White flag and take them by surprise. Girls on the outside, you will be captured but they can't tag everyone, so keep moving, no matter what, and one girl in the centre will eventually be able to take the flag – Good luck team.' Well, I was that centre girl and I captured the flag, which hadn't been by done by either team in ten years. When I was carried on the shoulders of the Blues, like a victor returning to Rome, I have never been so happy in my life, never felt so loved.

I loved camp – here I was in my element, I was like a wild animal finally able to release all its pent up aggression and surprisingly be rewarded for it with ribbons and trophies. The last year, when I was sixteen, I was told I was too old to return, so I wept on my final night. Tears dripped over my armful of prizes; to this day I cannot sing the goodbye camp song without having a nervous breakdown – (sung to the tune of 'Smoke Gets in Your Eyes'):

When camping days are through,
We'll remember you … Blue … team.
In sportsmanship and trust, you have been a must …

I tried to chain myself to the totem pole but they dug me out and returned me to real life. I was left with the most important lesson I ever learned thus far in life: beat the other team. Win at all costs. Conquer, conquer, conquer.

So when I returned to high school in the fall I felt ready to storm the inner sanctum, the spiritual realm of the rich Jewish Princesses. These uber-bitches of high school looked upon the rest of civilisation as worms. Clearly the Jews couldn't get near that concept in Austria but here in America, this first-generation Jew with rich parents was the master race: tall, tawny, imperious, with their Ralphie Lauren, million dollar skin and big blue eyes that looked like they'd been sucking on lemons for centuries. Even their noses seemed identical, thanks to the hard-working plastic surgeon, Dr Trilbey. They'd all gone from ethnic to Aryan in the bang of a hammer; the noses were flipped up so high some of them were actually face-to-face with their own nostrils – if they suddenly sneezed they could blind themselves.

Susie Grossmen, Didi Schwartz, Sidney Styler, I remember them so clearly, it's like I have them tattooed on my brain. With their shiny long black hair and perfect figures, they'd walk by me in the cafeteria – ass out, breasts pointed, the hands carried as if broken at the wrists like they were limp from the weight of future jewels. Cracking gum like a whip, 'Oh hi Shelley, Hi Debbie, Oh, like Alan is soooo cute. He has like this reeealy cool Corvette and I am like so jealous 'cause Tina's been pinned to him. I am like going to barf.'

Then they'd see me and I'd get a deadly, 'Oh hi.' Treating me like something that just died on the bottom of their shoe. Then they'd give a hair-flick and I'd get, 'Do you like look like that on purpose?' So I'd try to say something funny to get them to like me and the Princesses would go, 'I don't get it. That's like really stupid.' So I got funnier and funnier, how else is a small, flat-chested girl going to get some attention?

The really gorgeous girls at school had handmaidens, they were slightly uglier versions of themselves – one major defect and they were plummeted to the role of 'servant of gorgeous creature' whose main duties consisted of 'purse and gum carrier' – this is how, later in life, Princesses would treat their husbands. My mission was daunting but no mountain was too high for a girl who retained the glorious memory of having once captured the flag. I sized up the situation.

First, I made friends with the handmaidens, making them laugh and when they weren't looking I climbed up and up to the 'Perfect Bitches Nest'. Once I arrived, I pierced the heart of it and sucked its blood by befriending the most popular girl in the school, Norma Garel, also known, due to the enormity of her breast size, as Jugs. She was adorable, a cheerleader and she was mine.

Each night I would escape to her house where her mother held open the fridge door so I could experience what a fridge looked like with food in it – ours had mayonnaise from 1952, old lettuce, a used tea bag (my mother insisted we use it more than once), cigars and of course hot dogs. Then we'd close the fridge and her mother would give me warmth by feeding me meat loaf, and macaroni and cheese (love food).

Around this time my personality changed. Fuelled by early trauma, suddenly a latent turbo engine switched on inside me. In one night I went from Volkswagen to Ferrari, like someone from Las Vegas was inside me, moving my lips.

Overnight, I became the class comedian and found to my surprise I was suddenly valued by the very people who had spat on me. It was like growing tits overnight – I was a hit.

I must have learned to be 'funny' as a means of survival

from some primal part of my brain, otherwise where would the information come from? I'm sure the instinct to get funny dates back to primitive times when the tribe was about to sacrifice the weakest, most useless member and he suddenly thought, 'What the hell have I got to lose?' So he cracked the first joke. And as a result, the tribe thought, 'Wait a minute, he's worth keeping' and so the first comedian was saved from early extinction soup. Same with me.

And miracle of miracles, I got the boys. And once you got the boys, you got the girls – having the boys is like being given a lifetime supply of flypaper – popular girls volunteered to be my private gum carriers and Coke fetchers.

Now I raised my sights to new and dizzying heights; the Golden Boy, the WASP of all WASPS... Alan Wanzenberg.

Alan was the Robert Redford to my Barbra Streisand in *The Way We Were*. His hair was literally like gold, his eyes a deep blue. He was on the swim team with that body that was like an introverted triangle mounted on Adonis thighs and was destined to go to Harvard. He was accustomed to being ogled by the pointy babes. But I got him and now he too was mine.

Even my mother was ogling him. She would transform into a gibbering, flirtatious, girlie-girl. 'Oh, hello Alan can I get you a cookie?' No one, but no one, ever got a cookie in my house and she let him eat it with no plate underneath. He ate that cookie freefall, making crumbs and she didn't reach for her sponge. She just smiled provocatively. Even our dog Lumpi was made to use a napkin.

My allure for Alan was that I could make him laugh and show him a good time; every Friday night we would soar off in his green Triumph, passing the popular girls whose mouths hung open – I'd roll down the window and flash them the finger. We'd cruise to downtown Chicago where we'd regularly crash Hugh Hefner's parties, I'd ring the bell and on the doorstep would say that my father was at the party and could we come in and look for him, he was needed at home urgently. Alan would bring up the rear; once those women at the party clapped their eyes on him, the doors would fly open. I would like to think I emancipated him, released him from the bondage of his gorgeousness. His mother, a Master of WASPhood, called the school and asked them to keep him away from that 'Wax woman'.

But unlike the couple in love in *The Way We Were*, we weren't. Years later Alan turned gay on me, that's the twist in the tale. This is where I should have ridden into the sunset and lived happily ever after, but because of this cruel fate nature blew me, I had to build something else and it wasn't based on romance and love and family. So I re-routed and looking back, this was the first time I consciously drove off the motorway and chose a different direction from the route my life had been taking. My First Big Moment.

The happy couple.

The Austrian beauty.

Me – adorable and toothless.

The Mafia Don, his moll and their daughter.

Omi in front of her gold Cadillac.

Alpinian sheepherder at home.

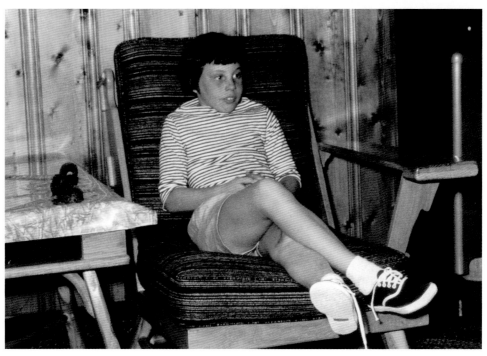

Freaked out in the basement (see page 23).

Jazz class with teeth (see page 31).

Lumpi and my father mid-hump.

4

MEN

'We know very little about the male. What do we know?
We know he's born, he grows a stomach, he dies.' Ruby Wax

MY RELATION TO RELATIONSHIPS was never good: even if
Alan-Golden-boy had been straight, we wouldn't have
survived. I was terrified of men and sent out an aura that said,
'Achtung! Verboten!' No one ever came near. I wasn't aware of
this sheath around me, so was constantly broken-hearted when
a potential boyfriend never called again. As a matter of fact the
day I started smoking, to kill myself, was the day Tommy

Banks, high school's second cutest guy, came to neck with me, got to mid-neck and left before the final hickie.

I was always the dumpee not the dumper – just once in my life I would have liked to say, 'Get out I never want to see you again!' Instead I've always had my teeth in the ankles on the way out the door; 'Please I'll change,' while gnawing at his socks, then perching on the telephone like an old budgie for the next 20 years, in case he calls back.

One summer, under protest, my parents made me skip summer camp; I was sent to finishing school in Switzerland at the prepubescent age of twelve. Pensionnat Violette was the crème de la crème of finishing schools, only the finest international young heirs were dispatched here, to straighten out any possible kinks. How sad my parents thought this top-dollar institution would have any influence on me; the beatings weren't working as well as my dad expected so he thought some strict, Swiss discipline might do the trick. My mother was still in the mindset that all Americans were wild, bronco-bucking cowboys. Pensionnat Violette, she hoped, would transform me into a sophisticated, educated, multilingual European like herself. She couldn't even straighten my teeth, so straightening my brain would take a miracle.

The school was reminiscent of the institution in the *Madeline* books. All the teachers were Miss Clavels, and the idea was 'in two straight lines we broke our bread and brushed our teeth and went to bed' – all except me.

I shared a room with eight little aristocratic girls. In the beginning they were stiff and well behaved, but with a little basic training I turned them into gum-chewing hoodlums. It became *Madeline: The Satanic Version*.

I was the 'Wild Woman from the West' who fucked with the system; years later I went back to visit and when I stuck my head in the front door I could hear the teachers screaming, 'RUBY THE TERRIBLE. SHE COMES.' 'RUBY THE TERRIBLE, SHE BACK.' I heard the distant sound of doors slamming; it was good to know I'd left my mark.

For the whole two months I refused to take a bath or change my clothes. I wore one red windbreaker and plaid skirt the whole time until it practically rotted on my flesh. On departure day, the girls all signed my red windbreaker, saying how much they'd miss me and how much fun they'd had and how much I smelled from the lack of washing, all in different languages.

Another rule was that we, the institutionalised, had to speak French in order to be fed. I overcame the problem without learning a word of French by repeating on a continuous loop, 'Frère Jacques, Frère Jacques, dormez-vous, dormez-vous', until they surrendered and gave me 'kwoissants', 'sauceyson', and 'ananan-as'.

Pets were at the top of the list of things forbidden. I remember sneaking a pregnant cat into the dorm and building it a nest out of toilet paper to keep it warm for its impending motherhood; the other girls were assigned milk and food runs. When I finally got busted for Possession of Cat I found out, to my disgust, it wasn't even female; it was just another male with a disease. The whole school had to be fumigated and put under quarantine.

Another time I opened the windows deliberately to let the bats in, to amuse myself: I enjoyed hearing the other girls scream – this is how I passed my time as I was banned, due to 'the cat incident', from all classes at this point. Sadly, my punishment was cleaning up the hundreds of pounds of bat shit the next day, but it was worth it to watch a whole army of Miss Clavels having to beat the bats from the rafters. But the climax of my stay was when I was inspired to dress up as a devil complete with horns, black cloak and pitchfork. I assigned Anita, the girl who shared my bunk, to be my counterpart, an angel – she had no choice.

I remember spending hours lavishing attention on her, making her crepe-paper wings, sculpting a halo out of tin foil and creating the most beatific, angelic make-up job on her face. Then – and I can't exactly remember why – I sent her off into the streets of Montreux as a little golden-haired angel while I headed in the opposite direction as the dark-haired,

red-faced devil. I probably just stuck my head in some *boulan-geries* and shouted 'Boo', but when I came back to the school, there was mayhem. I saw a blur of grown-ups running back and forth, using some strange guttural language and shoving me angrily out of the way. No one would tell me what was going on, the children didn't know and the adults weren't telling. I never found out officially, but to this day I have an image burned into my mind – I look through the keyhole of the bathroom door, Anita floats in the bathtub. Her paper wings have wilted around her, halo concertinaed down over her face and her lipstick is smeared up to her forehead. Her eyes are dead looking. The devil part of me knew something bad had happened to her.

My mother had instilled in me I was born evil and on this memorable night I felt it and couldn't have been in a better outfit. Several days later my mother arrived to take me away. It never occurred to me that I had been kicked out of Pensionnat Violette: it's only recently dawned on me that I was the only one leaving that day.

My next inkling of sexuality was at 13. I was standing in Chicago in a record shop, when I had my first sighting of a psychedelic poster, Jimi Hendrix's head under an infrared light making the neon, Day-Glo colours take on that that acid burning, 'if drugs can do this I'm going to try it' effect. Over the speakers The Beatles were singing 'Well she was just seventeen' and all of my organs lit up into red alert. This was the most excit-ing sound I had ever heard – It Was A Big Moment. No one man since then has ever switched the 'on' button like they did.

After that I covered my bedroom walls in Beatles posters that I ritually licked. I would turn up the sound of my Beatles records to eardrum-shattering levels and weep and moan and scream out my love. I collected every single Beatles magazine, pen, poster, record, sunglasses, chocolate, alarm clock, socks, food, stamp, sticker … you name it, if it had The Beatles' name on it, I bought it. I sometimes called the operator in Liverpool just to hear her say 'Hello' in that accent, then I'd become so overwhelmed I'd have to hang up. My mother approved of my dedication because she hoped it meant I would never sleep with a real person. Also it was easy to wipe down the posters and it kept me at home.

So when it was announced The Beatles were coming to Chicago in 1967, my mother bought the tickets for both shows, one at noon and one at night. I loved Paul the most – I was ready to give myself to him but first I had to look like Jane Asher. I studied his girlfriend's photos, her clothes and what she looked like. I had to straighten my hair so I plugged in the iron – no one told me you were supposed to put a cloth between the iron and your hair, most of my crispy hairs dropped out, leaving a couple of burnt knots on my scalp. In the end, four remain-ing hairs jutted out from beneath my plastic John Lennon hat.

In the photos, Jane liked hip-hugging mini-skirts. These did not exist in Chicago at the time but, undeterred, I borrowed my mother's skirt, left the zipper wide open and wore it from mid thigh down. It was secured with a girdle I also borrowed from mama and folded the top of it over the skirt to hold it in place; the girdle was fully visible, like a belt.

In this condition, I chased The Beatles' limo when they arrived at Chicago O'Hare Airport, flinging myself across their windshield as my mother screamed from behind me, 'Go Ruby, Go!' As the concert was at White Sox Baseball Stadium, I just screamed along with 25,000 other hysterical girls going through the white heat of puberty.

After the first show, I hatched my plan; I noticed that The Beatles exited through a dugout which was presumably where their dressing room was. When the evening show started, I stayed for the first song, then cleverly sneaked off to the dugout to wait for my betrothed, Paul. Annoyingly, I found myself followed by four other fat, sad, hairless, girdled girls and we all hid in the shower together. Before getting into the shower stall, I went around touching the toilet lids because I believed they had Beatles germs on them. (I thought men always sat down on toilets at that point in my life.) Then I joined the fat losers, and we stood in that shower stall for God knows how long – we didn't know how much time went by as we were panting with excitement.

Gradually, we realised the screaming had stopped, so we hesitantly emerged wondering where our dream boys were. The stadium was empty and dark, there was silence only broken by my mother's voice shouting, 'Vooby vooby ver are you?' We missed the whole show; The Beatles had been airlifted by helicopter to their next city, but it set me on a mission to come to England. I never had such a huge mission before, now I had one – I thought I would come to England, find Paul and he would save me from my life.

There is a happy ending to this story (unlike much of the rest of this book). This last year I was on stage for the finale of the Queen's Jubilee and I'm standing to the right of Paul McCartney who starts to sing 'Well she was just seventeen'. I have friends who saw me on television with my hands over my mouth, weeping. I'd gone on such a long journey to finally be this close to the man of my dreams. A little voice from the playground suddenly piped up, 'How the hell did you pull this off, Ruby?' This is where your mind takes a snapshot and you think, I could die happy now.

Afterwards at Buckingham Palace I was overexcited and spotted Paul. I made my way over to tell him about my moment on stage with him. I opened my mouth and he starts in with that accent, 'You've no idea what tonight was for me.' (I thought for a second he was talking about seeing me.) 'I was twelve,' he went on, 'and I'd won an essay competition and I got to meet the Queen Mother at the last Jubilee and I was so nervous. Tonight I'm up there singing and the Queen comes onstage personally to thank me.' He'd definitely won the contest of 'How the hell did I get here?' I didn't even bother with my story.

But I digress; I was 'just seventeen' when my parents made one last attempt to civilise me. Most parents would have given up, but not them. I'd been at Camp Agawak for the last few summers, which turned me into a champion canoeist, but I don't think this is what they dreamt of for me. So they sent me off to another Swiss finishing school on Lake Geneva. A row of luxury mansions stood on either side of the school, immediately to our right was Brigitte Bardot's villa, which had a steady stream of gentlemen callers. My roommate, who was also seventeen, was the younger version of Gina Lollobrigida: she would loll on her bed moaning for a man in a sexy Italian accent. So, obligingly I went onto our wrap-around balcony and flagged some men over who were on their way to see Brigitte. I realised then I had a gift: I was a natural born pimp. Oh, and I never learned French.

Driven by my obsession, I ran away from this school to meet my amour, Paul, who I imagined was waiting for me in London even if he didn't know it himself. My escape was inspired by the film *Pollyanna* starring Hayley Mills; I tied bedsheets together and crawled down from the balcony to a waiting taxi, which took me to the airport. Then I flew to London.

On arrival I hit the King's Road, wheeling my big red suit-case behind me. All the shops were decorated with trapeze, merry-go-rounds, go-go lighting … oh, and by the way, they sold clothes. At Stop-the-Shop (so called because it rotated) I talked a friendly salesgirl into letting me stay at her house.

She lived in a full-frontal Chelsea Pad with that black and white chequered floor, beanbag chairs, hanging beds, hookahs and hash pipes. It was more disco than house. Unbelievably adorable, Beatle-moptopped men in their collarless jackets would come over day and night and take us to parties, rock concerts and happenings. But one thing I will never, never understand is with all that sexual freedom why, oh why, did not one man attempt to have sex with me? (See aura, again.) People were having sex with their pets, for God's sake, and not one man of any description tried to get me to bed.

After a while, I wired my parents for money and my parents wired back: one dollar. Finally, my mother flew over and I was summoned to the Dorchester Hotel where she waited for me in the lobby, did a verbal aria accompanied by hard slapping and dragged me into the taxi.

I blanked out a lot of what happened around now.

But a year later, back in London I finally lost my virginity. I conned my parents into sending me to summer school to study literature at Cambridge, ha ha. I didn't waste a second; I escaped straight to Hyde Park and picked up a busker. He had all the requirements for my first fling. He was the lookalike of Paul McCartney – I've always said, 'If you can't get the real thing, get the body double.' I told him I had a place for him to crash, which I didn't. Instead, I took him to a hotel where I asked at the main desk for my room key, pointing to a hook marked 1345 – I'd never been in this hotel before but luckily they handed over the key that was hanging there. I never considered that someone could have been staying in the room.

So I took my Paul McCartney lookalike to room 1345, where he attempted penetration. It was so painful for me, I threw him across the room where he landed in a heap. The next morning the maid came to clean the room expecting it to be empty and reported us to the manager. Up he came and threatened to call the police. I decided to play 'dumb American', protesting I didn't understand about this 'checking in procedure', that I thought you just picked a room and paid for it afterwards. I looked so innocent and young – the manager let me go. Then the newly disabled Paul Lookalike and I moved to a slum dwelling in Queensway, where overnight I developed asthma from the dust and had to be taken to hospital by ambulance. Remarkably, I never heard from him again. My life ... so romantic.

As usual, I needed money and my parents said as usual 'no'.

By popular demand I was required back in Evanston to complete the final year of my useless high school education. I arrived, saturated in hormone juice. At this point, I started to smoke dope every day so my story gets a little patchy here – as a matter of fact, I don't remember much at all.

(Blank, blank, blank.)

Now began 'the dead years'. During this time I vaguely remember windows and sneaking out of them to see the musical *Hair*. I must have gone to see it over 134 times. Remember the guy in the show who I stalked? After the shows we'd go to his slum dwelling where he would attempt sex. I didn't get the manual as to what the procedures were for intercourse, but more importantly parental guidance made sure I would never open my legs wilfully, so Ken started to lose interest. Surprised? Even though he couldn't complete a sentence (he used to answer my questions with some words and then hum for the rest: I'd say, 'Ken what's going on?' He'd answer, 'Well, you know da di da di da,'), I was obsessed with him and when I didn't just show up, would phone after every show. I used to say, my voice shaking, 'Is Ken there?' I could hear him whisper on the other end, 'Tell her I'm not here.' But I refused to take 'no' for an answer even though he quickly got another slut/girlfriend. One New Year's Eve my parents sent the police out to find me – I was discovered in Ken's closet, stoned out of my mind. He was with the slut.

My parents threatened me that unless I dropped him immediately and went to university to feed my mind, I would be forever cut off from the Kingdom of Sausages. Denver University took me at very short notice. In my final year of high school I had applied to every university in America and had been rejected by all of them except New York University. My father happened to be in New York when someone blew up their parents' townhouse. It seems there were three students in the basement making bombs and one radical revolutionary accidentally detonated one. A boy was killed and the other two girls went into hiding – it happens, I tried to tell my father.

Anyway, because my father was frightened I'd become a revolutionary, New York University was now *verboten* so I was shipped westward.

As far as I could make out, people went to Denver University to major in joint rolling, so it was perfect for me. I was determined to spend my time there constructively – my days and nights were filled with getting blitzed, rioting and partaking in street violence. Luckily, the Vietnam War was going on so we had an inbuilt excuse for anarchy, but the truth is I just wanted to throw a bomb or maim someone in authority … I was that angry.

I had some rich student friends, also angry at their parents, who were planning as an act of protest (only to their parents) to blow up a bank in New York. They took a taxi and were still arguing about the plans in the back seat, while the cab driver drove them straight to the police station, I think they're still in prison. Such times we had.

Inevitably, we closed down the school to cover the campus in tents, A-frames and geodesic domes; we called it Woodstock West. We pretended it was a political statement but really it was just an excuse to have a party, stop having to go to boring school, and fuck with the system. It was the only thing I got to fuck with at that time ... no, that's not quite true, there was a nice boy called Tom Feldman whom I brutalised in the end for being kind to me; I had problems with the male, what can I say? Tom, if you're reading this, I'm really sorry.

(Blank, blank.)

But I know, looking back in my records, I did one year at Denver, two months at Berkeley University, sold mescalin to get to Europe, went with faggot friend who dumped me in Israel to take acting lessons, ended up in a bedsit in London for two years getting fatter and fatter, was rejected from all drama schools except one which must have been desperate: the Royal Scottish Academy of Music and Drama in the heart of down-town Glasgow.

A mere six years after Tom, I managed to get another boyfriend. In this amount of time, your hymen can almost grow together again. There he was in voice class, I spotted him immediately, a Paul McCartney lookalike. James Fleet was scrawny, with those lanky limbs, Beatle moptop and those angelic, moony eyes. I know this sounds weird, but there was also a girl in my class who had the sexy look of John Lennon. They both fought over me. This was beyond my wildest dreams. I found Alison incredibly sexy and really wanted to be a lesbian but the old hormones just wouldn't play ball. So in the end I chose Paul. I'm pretty sure we had a good time, but I can't swear to it.

(Blank, blank, blank.)

What I can remember clearly was my father's response after meeting him. 'Drop him, he's a nothing, and will never amount to anything. He must be a fairy.'

These days you can catch James Fleet in *Four Weddings and a Funeral*, about 20 films and various other successful television series. After drama school I never heard from Jamie again and assumed he dropped me. Last year, when I sold my parents' house in Chicago, I was going through my mother's suitcase and found stacks of his love letters claiming undying love and begging me to respond, letters I had never received. By the way, there were other love letters from boys which my mother had also secretly hoarded; boys I assumed brutally dropped me.

Two years after drama school and endless command appearances at Evanston, I auditioned for Mel Smith, the then artistic director of the Crucible Theatre, Sheffield. Mel was incredibly magnetic, brilliant and funny; that was the glue.

When my father first clapped eyes on him, in the foyer of the National Theatre, he shouted in front of everyone, 'Oh, my God, Ruby this is perversion of nature. This man is a monster. He'll never amount to anything.' My father followed up with calls day and night making sure the 'monster' was out of my life. I didn't literally drop Mel but my father had lit a fuse to curse the relationship.

The pressure was relentless – I eventually drove Mel away.

P.S. Daddy, today Mel is worth many millions. He is a successful actor/director, all from never amounting to anything.

Once Mel departed I shut down for many years. I was so battle-weary, that I decided to devote my late twenties and early thirties to a man who could never harm me – a homosexual, Michael. Brilliant, huh?

Let me set the record straight: living with a fag is a no-win situation but you can have a lot of laughs. We share the same sense of humour and the same taste in genitalia. There is some good news: he's neat and can tell you what goes with what, clothes-wise. However, he cannot change a light bulb nor is he, to be blunt, great at sex. When I tell you how hard I worked on this guy, the hours I had to manipulate him with nothing going on – I can only say I developed incredible right arm muscles. Eventually you realise no matter what you do, you will never turn him on. One day, while making the bed, I found a stack of gay magazines filled with erect penises and I knew I could never compete with that. But knowing the alternative was to have to go out with straight men I thought I'd swallow this. (Pun intended.) I finally got my father what he always feared, the phantom fairy. He put a fatwah on Michael. 'He's a nothing and will never amount to anything.' He spewed directly into Michael's face on their first meeting. *Note*: Michael became executive vice president of a large corporation – however, it is true he was a fairy.

And for my final act, I'd like to tell you about my last boyfriend before I found the good news, my husband Ed. After Michael I started to think maybe my father was right. I should go for a straight man preferably with money. Back in London, I started dressing up like a Femme Fatale; full make-up, tight skirts, clicky-click heels. For a woman who'd always dressed like a little man up till this point, this new ensemble made me feel like a transvestite. Bravely, I cruised wine bars in the City, waiting for someone to come up to me and say, 'Please marry me.' I guessed that was how you picked up someone normal. But without the facility to flirt, I ended up talking to the wait-ers, who found me enchanting. I couldn't come on to these testosterone-fuelled men in their striped suits, yabbering about the stock exchange and glugging champagne; their dominant genes frightened me.

Finally, at a film party, I captured my alpha male. He was

rich, elegant, handsome and – guess what? – reminded me of my father. (See my father as Charles Boyer.) I hit the jackpot, I thought. When he was introduced, I did everything I could to curb my usual impulses (which entailed out-butching the man in question and competing with him till he screamed for mercy). This time I shut the fuck up and smiled sweetly, I let him treat me like I was a 'girl'. When he sent me chocolates from Belgium and roses from Harrods, I started to feel like I'd been miscast in a sitcom. We went to dinner and I let him order for me and I became a kept woman. He gave me the key to his mews, and a list of what I should buy at Fortnum & Mason; he assumed I was there to cater to his every whim. The sex was brutal and after our first night of hard humping, he told me to lose weight.

I accepted his invitation to the Cannes Film Festival and let him dress me in the style he thought appropriate; he bought me skirts and little stewardess jackets, clutch bags and girly lingerie. At the hotel in Cannes, he told me to keep the bed warm while he did meetings. At his business dinners I pretended he was more interesting than me. – Can you imagine? I even cheered him when he went jogging in the morning waving a handkerchief as he trotted off. He thought of me as his 'petite femme' and often spoke French to me, which he hadn't noticed I didn't speak – he knew nothing about me. Finally, he gave me a biography of his father who was a famous writer. By page 50 I thought how similar our backgrounds were. By page 79 the book mentioned that his mother had made a pass at his sister and by page 85 the sister had shot herself in the head, it started to dawn on me that maybe our lives weren't similar after all. By page 150, I'd learnt that his father had to screw at least 15 women a day to keep his creative juices flowing – if the work was going particularly well they serviced him while he typed. Had I perhaps chosen the wrong Mr Right?

I finally flipped at his half-sister's engagement party. We were at a resort in France where I broke into an insane tirade – this monologue which I thought was hilarious did not get the expected round of applause from the dead-eyed French party guests. My sugar daddy looked at me as if I had just slipped from Ms Jekyll to Ms Hyde. He whipped his front-door key out of my hand and so ended the relationship and with it my dream of being a kept woman. 'La Femme Captive.'

5

AMBITION:
THE ROAD TO SUCCESS

'Success is getting what you want. Happiness is wanting what you get.' Dostoyevsky

CELEBRITY IS A FANTASTIC SUBSTITUTE for mommy and daddy's fuck-ups. Usually if you scratch the surface of anyone attracted to the limelight you'll find some kid in the playground who never made the hop-scotch team. Dysfunction breeds need for celebrity, otherwise it serves no purpose except for the privilege

75

of having drunks and weirdos come over and belch how much they love you. To a normal person this would be intolerable.

I'd already created a pretty large persona: a hyper-driven, turbo-engined improvement on the original nerd (see playground). It's the remake of the ugly duckling story, only I didn't turn into a swan – I turned into Joan Rivers. Yes, thanks to the anthrax of my home front I decided to pursue a career in acting. Which was a remarkable decision considering I had no talent and wasn't exactly wowing them in the looks department.

I informed my father when I was about 14 of my destiny. He wanted to celebrate by taking me to dinner (I should have known) with the incredibly famous comedian Henny Youngman, renowned for his classic joke, 'Hey waiter, there's a fly in my soup.' Are you laughing …? Anyway we go out and he's brought his opening act along with him to dinner, some schmuck magician who kept making his shoe appear on his soup plate.

After we ate, my father told him with a smirk, 'Ruby wants to be a comedian.' I had not said a peep up to this point. Henny made me stand up and circle the table like he could see if I'm funny by the way I walk. Then he smacks me in the head and declares, 'Maybe she should go into PR.' Years later, when I was doing the Montreal Comedy Festival, Henny was the MC. He was pretty senile at the time and was facing in the wrong direction, but introduced me. As I passed him on the stage I hit him hard in the head and said, 'Maybe you should go into PR.' Of course he had no idea what I was talking about but it made me feel good ... Oh, PS. My comedy act was awful so maybe I should have gone into PR.

In high school I auditioned for *Hello, Dolly!*, which was the big play of the year. The whole school got in but me. There were 6,000 people in the cast; I remember perusing the endless cast list, and realising I was excluded, I almost threw up on my shoes. This stoked my sense of revenge. There was a gang that were the theatricals of Evanston High, the 'Thespians of Suburbia'. They were so confident and sure that they would end up successful. I followed their demise after graduation with the relish of a snake watching the rat after it bites it and it dies; I always kept abreast of their failure in the coming years. There was the Mary Tyler Moore of the bunch, who could sing, dance and act. She was the 'It' girl at 17 and we always thought she would be a hit on Broadway. She headed straight for New York University Fine Arts Program and we expected great things from her. I waited, recoiled. Then I heard she caught Lyme's Disease and couldn't work again. I commiserated at the time and gave out lines like, 'Oh, that's awful, she was so talented.' Aren't I a bitch?

PS. The rest of them are serving sentences at various community dinner theatres, i.e. the Boothby Players in Maine where you serve lobster, put a bib on the customer and then tap your way through 'Ain't Misbehavin''.

My first phase of revenge involved learning to act: I would outshine them all, if only I knew what a play looked like. I got the list from the 'Thespians of Suburbia' of the best drama schools in the country. I then auditioned for every one of them and was rejected one by one. The court was unanimous ... I stank. But that didn't stop me so I took a summer school course in Shakespearean acting at Berkeley University, all you had to do to get in there was pay.

Every sad, fat, only child was on this course, each more appalling than the next. The teacher made us do really helpful acting exercises, things like telling us to imagine we were getting smaller and smaller until we imploded. Finally he thought we were ready for performance. He would only allow us to do small scenes, since directing us in a whole play would be intolerable.

I played Ophelia to a large Jamaican non-English-speaking person's Hamlet. Take Moby Dick and stick him in a jerkin – that's what my co-star looked like. When he bowed it was a miracle he didn't smother in his own cellulite. Luckily, you couldn't understand a word either of us was saying, otherwise Shakespeare would rise from the dead and slice us in twain with a rapier. He recited an incomprehensible, 'To be or not to be ...' People in the audience were asking what he was supposed to be … or not be? It could have been anything – a train, a giraffe, a toffee.

I entered and didn't know anything except I was supposed to be sad, so I started sobbing over my 'Oh what a noble mind …' speech, distorted by the running mucus, while tears rolled down my convulsed face. On my last line, waiting for the applause (I thought the silence meant I was delivering a masterpiece), I got in a foetal position and lay in a pool of self-indulgence. I expected a standing ovation when I was done but saw only stunned faces.

After the performance, I came out to find my father hidden behind a tree. 'If you ever go on that stage again,' he said, 'I will beat you senseless.' I knew then that I would become an actress.

I also knew in a haze of self-delusion that since no one in America recognised my talents, I should go to England and become a classical actress based on my magificent performance in Shakespeare. Are you getting how misguided I was?

I was nineteen at the time and thought, how can I raise some money and get myself over to England? What could I possibly sell that there was a need for at this particular time? In my capitalist fibres I understood the concept of supply and demand. So I came up with it – sell drugs. I was in the right place, Berkeley, where they specialised in drug-making, what a lucky break. I asked a friend in the biochemist lab to make me

2,000 tabs of acid and sold them with the enthusiasm and good-sportsmanship with which I'd once sold girl scout cookies.

Back when I was a girl scout there was a reward incentive: if we sold over 200 boxes, we received a badge of an appliquéd cookie. I remember accosting old ladies and ramming peanut butter cookies into their toothless gums, holding a girl scout knife to their jugular and screaming, 'Swallow you bitch.' What I lacked in talent I made up for in competitiveness.

So when it came to drugs, I was a natural. The Hell's Angels considered a bulk order and asked me what kind of acid I was selling. I made up a name on the spot: 'St Louis Bluies' (I was new to the field). In fact I'd had only taken acid twice myself. Once was on an unforgettable trip to Disneyland where my friends had to whack me over the head to get me home, I was removed from several rides for becoming over-emotional. I crawled out of the barge in Small, Small World to make friends with all the moving puppets from around the world, I wanted to live in harmony among them as I hulaed with the Hawaiian dolls and rubbed noses with the Eskimos and then was manhandled out the side door by two Disney heavies. On Pirates of the Caribbean I completely lost it: I thought they were trying to kill me with a canon. I screamed at the shooting pirates until Security turned off the ride. They even gave us a refund, which is unheard of at Disney in the little-known area called Kingdom of Refunds. About ten miles out of Disneyland I shouted to my friends, 'Stop the car, I'm getting on this ride,' waving my ticket book. I ran at some gasworks, thinking they were another ride in Futureworld.

The other time I dropped acid was in a small town in Mexico. My friends and I travelled 27 hours to get to this festival of the Punta Yaya or something; when we got there an old, parched taco maker offered me a ladleful of Mescal, which I think is the organic version of mescalin. I swallowed a mouthful and woke up three days later lying in the street with a hoof mark on my hair – I had missed the festival.

I made enough money to go to Europe with a friend, Blake, from the Chicago cast of *Hair*. Now we've all seen and heard the shtick of queens. Back when I was nineteen Blake was my first encounter with a true homosexual genius. Sex didn't turn me on but his mental acrobatics did. He was fast and funny and as he served those one-liners, I could fling them back. We played like two Wimbledon champions until we were driven into a frenzy of hysteria. As a matter of fact, on our travels he made me laugh so much I got bronchitis and ended up in an oxygen tent in Spain. I could have died laughing, which isn't a bad end.

At home, my parents had forbidden me to speak to Blake. Mother: 'This is a bum, a schlemiel, who'll bring you down to the gutter.' My father would tear the phone from the wall and threaten to beat me senseless. What's ironic is Blake was the only person I knew at that time who didn't take drugs. The friends they encouraged me to have in high school were often found lying face down in their own vomit from a night of snorting Demerol. My father forbade me to ever see or speak to this 'Homo fairy' again.

This was enough of a reason to choose Blake as my fellow traveller. My dream was to join the Living Theatre, presently touring Europe; we would follow in their footsteps. What I loved about their style was that they wore gas masks and shouted 'Fuck you' in many languages into the bewildered faces of the audience. They were always naked, flapping their genitals angrily and screaming, 'You napalmed 20,000 gooks you fuckheads!' Then released balloons, which symbolised … something. This was it for me; a lot of aggression could be released in the name of art. We found out they were to be performing in Barcelona so we hitchhiked from London through France towards Spain. These were days when you could actually arrive at your destination without being cut into bite-sized chunks and then eaten. Instead, generous people would pick you up, take you home, feed you, share their dope and then let you out again – alive.

At a party we crashed in St Tropez, a man proposed to me because I looked like the replica of his girlfriend, who had died in a plane crash. Since he was an Alain Delon lookalike, I almost stuck around – two lookalikes, that's better than most people get in a lifetime.

When we got to Barcelona I found out the Living Theatre had been arrested while still in South America and were languishing in a jail in Peru, or so the posters read. I was devastated. We went to the nearest airport and Blake, to cheer me up, asked me where was the last place on earth I'd like to go? I said Israel, so he immediately bought me a one-way ticket and abandoned me. Fags! It was his idea of a joke. I never saw him again.

The only thing about flying to Israel was I knew my best friend from high school was there working on a kibbutz: Norma Garel (aka Jugs) was being a good Jewish girl. My parents were dry heaving with happiness when I told them I was in Israel and said they would now send me money to support this new habit and the fact I was with Norma enhanced their ecstasy. When I got to 'Ramahazagankan' or whatever it's called, I hated it. I quickly realised I would not be bending over to pluck radishes for Jews for free, which is the Big Scam of the kibbutz.

The only good time I had at the slave labour camp was the night Jugs and I got stoned and cheered wildly as we watched fireworks over Lebanon. The next day we found we had been watching the beginning of the Six Day War. We swore never to take drugs again. I left her happy in the trenches, cheerfully fucking the locals and I departed for Tel Aviv.

Money was running out and I knew if I didn't think fast I

would have to return to Auschwitz, I mean, Evanston and live with Mommy and Daddy. This filled me with such terror that I decided to become a serious actress in the Royal Shakespeare Company. If I could get in there I would be safe in Stratford. Remember I had absolutely no talent, a very obnoxious American accent and a fat ass. I phoned Tel Aviv University and asked for the number of a drama coach. Avid, an over-the hill leading man type, offered to let me stay in his house and said he'd coach me for my drama school auditions in London. We started with theatre exercises where he made me imagine I was getting smaller and smaller until I imploded. After months of imaginatively imploding, he thought *Yes she's ready* to play Juliet.

For three months in his living room, I worked on my Juliet speech. I knew what she ate for breakfast, what she wore, what she thought – I learned to be Juliet. The only problem was I couldn't act like Juliet, but this didn't stop me. Off I went to London to seek my fortune with a shitty audition piece in my pocket and no chance of getting into drama school. But reality had never gotten in my way before.

Father wrote 'Come home immediately, you'll only end up broken-hearted. Millions of girls try to be actresses and only one in a billion make it. You're a simple girl so come home, don't be so crazy.'

Mother wrote 'You're too fat to be an actress. Lose weight,

I know what's best for you. I'm your mother, I only say this because I love you.'

To know what London was like, see the film *Austin Powers*. Everyone around me was having an orgy – I was on the sidelines, watching. Maybe it was because I wore a coat made of goat. When it rained, I smelt like a farm decomposing – it wasn't any better when the coat came off. I was covered in tie-dye, looking like an alien had shat on me; bellbottoms that made me look even shorter and squatter than I was; and on top, my hair was frazzled. I looked like an angry, hairy little man. Albert Einstein without the beard; a dwarf dictator covered in beads, bells, peace and love badges.

In contrast, every London girl was a dolly bird, equipped with mini-skirt, cut up above the vagina line, spaghetti length, long legs, toes pointed inward to make them look like they had the mind of a tadpole and big eyelashes that looked like spiders trying to escape.

Thinking about it, they weren't so much like dolly birds, they were more like a spinal cord in a skirt.

My parents' cash flow had dried up. I called home by reverse charge to explain that my new plan was to go legit, enter a drama school for three years and then hopefully work in the theatre – the Royal Shakespeare Company actually. There was a long pause. Then my father said 'How much?' At the time, drama school was about a hundred pounds a term. I could hear some scratching and whispering, it was my parents calculating how much drama school would cost for three years, subtracted from how much a mental institution in Chicago would cost for the same amount of time. Also, adding in the exchange rates. I heard them suppress a chuckle when they came to the bit about me having a job in the theatre. After a while they came back with an affirmative. I was delirious with happiness, as I smelled freedom. If I could support myself as an actress, I might never have to go home again.

My parents kept me on the poverty line with just enough to make me dependent on them but not comfortable. I lived on muesli, which you could buy by the barrel and stuffed myself with it to drown out the loneliness of living alone. Eventually my ass became the size of a small motor home. When I walked I could hear myself crunch but at least I could hear I existed. I lived in a godforsaken bedsit with red, purple and yellow paisley carpet and matching walls – like the room had haemorrhaged. You had to constantly feed the meter 50p and when you forgot you'd be plunged into darkness. My only heat source was those flickering orange, fibreglass coals – no heat came from them, only flickering. I used to straddle my hair dryer for warmth and if you wanted a shower you had to crouch in the silverfish-infested tub and hold a nozzle above your head as a driblet of water would scald, freeze, scald, freeze its way onto your scalp.

HOW DO YOU WANT ME?

The room reminded me of English films in the Fifties with drippy-drip teakettles; everyone had runny noses, cloth coats, bad abortions and then hung themselves in the end. Outside it was swinging London, everyone was having sex with Mick, Keith, John and Paul, except me. Even Yoko Ono, for God's sake, a woman who sang like a thousand cats being castrated. You couldn't even see her, actually, she was wall-to-wall hair, it was like the woman was carpeted and this is before she wore a windshield across her eyes, before she looked like a Toyota driving at you. And what did she do to capture a Beatle? She hammered a nail in a fucking cloud.

Of course, I never forayed outside except to forage for food and once to visit a shrink, who gave me a prescription for Valium to calm me down. I thought if I just endlessly concentrated on Juliet, on my knees, eating cereal, I would finally become her. Once RADA recognised my transformation, they would welcome me with open arms and then my life would begin.

Note: I had used this type of concentration once before when I was about ten. I thought if I didn't eat or sleep I'd figure out how to turn myself invisible. I would use my dog to experiment on. So after a few days of sleep deprivation, starvation and thinking really hard, I came up with an idea, but it was insane: if I painted my dog with enough layers of clear nail polish, he wouldn't actually be invisible, but at least, he could pass as a blur.

So in a similar mindset of madness I studied being Juliet day and night. But here was the genius of the plan. Rather than starving, I would eat and eat enough muesli till I was really fat. A fat Juliet – very few other people can say, 'I crammed for Juliet.' By this point I believed I was her and in the worst English accent in the world, started to use 'thee' 'my liege' 'zounds' and 'fear not' in my everyday speech. Did I mention I wore a wimple? It was the only thing that fit.

Finally, after seven months of total immersion in one speech I felt ready for my audition. I entered the gothic hallowed halls that reminded me of a haunted house and gave my name among other shaking hopefuls. I was called unto the stage. Gasping for breath, I introduced myself, 'Juliet from *Romeo and Juliet* by Sir William Shakespeare – the Bard.' I went to centre stage and then proceeded to get into the mood. I was doing the speech where Juliet panics because she thinks Romeo is dead. So, I tried to get myself emotionally in the moment by saying to myself, 'My dog is dead. My dog is dead,' but I started to say it aloud in my nervousness so you can imagine how confused the auditioners were, 'Did Juliet have a dog?' I thought I heard someone mumble. The only sound you could hear was my own sobbing and moaning about loving my pet dog Lumpi so much and why did he have to die?

I knew it was going to be difficult to understand what I was saying, what with the accent and the sobbing – which I anticipated, so I brought out my *pièce de resistance*, a prop. In the speech, Juliet, to show how crazy she's gotten, threatens to beat out her brains with Tybalt's bone. Tybalt is her dead cousin (it's a metaphor) but nobody told me. To help me out visually, I got out a whole fresh turkey leg purchased from the butcher's that morning, and brandished it at the end of the monologue. One last 'My dog is dead' and I sink to my knees head down – head jerks up abruptly as I fix the darkness with a crazed stare.

'Alack, alack it is not like that I, what with loathsome smells [I sniff the air crazily] and shrieks [I shriek like my mother], like mandrakes torn out of the earth that living mortals hearing them run mad. [I mime pulling big clumps of hair from my head.] Oh, if I wake, shall I not be distraught and madly play with my forefather's joints? [I play vaguely with some invisible joints.] And pluck the mangled Tybalt from his shroud? [I make plucking movements high in the air.] And in this rage, with some great kinsman's bone, as with a club, dash out my desperate brains.' I take out the turkey bone and mime hitting myself over the head. I then collapse on the floor in a heap and wait for the applause. There was none.

I was told to go into a classroom and wait to see who would make the callbacks. A goateed man in a black turtleneck entered and read some names, but not mine. When I asked if there was some mistake, he said, 'I don't think so,' and turned away.

I stood outside the doors of RADA and swallowed a bottle of Valium, which sadly only contained three pills. Feeling better, I marched back in again and asked the registrar if she knew anyone who could help me act. I got the number of Virginia Snyders, who gave private lessons. I called and begged and begged till she took pity and invited me to her home in Maida Vale. She must have spotted perhaps not great talent, but a person who so deeply wanted something from her – to keep her out of Evanston.

She cut me a deal: I would Hoover my mentor's floors and she would teach me Chekhov. Sadly, her floors never really got clean, but then again I never really got Chekhov. But I was so driven, I could finally pass off, whatever it was I was doing, as acting.

I applied to every drama school in England and was unanimously turned down. Finally I jumped ship and applied to Glasgow, I'd had to find another landmass that might take me. The competition was nonexistent – who in their right mind wanted to go to school in Glasgow? Back in the Seventies it was like an ashtray with stoplights: the buildings were blackened, the sky was blackened and pink garbage bags were left on the street to add some colour. Now, of course, it's the cultural centre of Europe – improvement always happens once I leave. On the way to school you had to hurtle over the bodies of homeless drunks, it was fantastic exercise. Glasgow was a mess and it was perfect for me. It looked on the outside how I felt on the inside – chaos, anger and anarchy. What I loved about the Scots, though, was their national pride; ordinary people were knowledgeable about battles and other historical facts. I remember one taxi driver telling me about why they wear kilts. I can't really remember the details:

There was a battle in … somewhere. And one clan was jealous of the other clan's tartan. They both wanted the Burberry pattern because they knew one day Americans would demand it on the inside of their raincoats and they would make a fortune out of it. Anyway both clans put on their blue zigzag eye shadow and charged at each other down the mountain. As they were leaping from rock to rock, they tore their golf slacks at the crotch – so I think it was Old Mel McGibson who said, 'I know let's wear skirts, we're in the middle of nowhere who's going to find out.' And as a joke he said, 'No underpants.' As for the sporran, the hairier men had so much excess hair, they shaved their calves, glued the residue onto their handbags and wore them as fanny packs.

This might not be accurate.

And now a little description of the school: imposing, Victorian grandeur with big sweeping staircases and dignified high-backed wooden chairs. Some of the students were deeply ungifted and some were as talented as I was. (Interpret this how you will.) Just to give you a flavour of what got in, there was Aaron, a chunk of Scottish meat with those big dribbly red lips. For the audition we had to select a famous Shakespearian monologue from a list the school provided. Aaron chose the Hamlet speech: 'To be or not to be … with a bare bodkin.' This was my second exposure to a Shakespearian massacre – on the list they'd just written the first and last line of the speech and to show you the calibre of Aaron's brain, that's all he performed. He stood in front of the audition panel and delivered the lines: 'To be or not to be, "Dot", "dot", "dot". With a bare bodkin.' Then he bowed and exited … he got in.

We also had Allie, a gypsy so sexy you almost forgot that she couldn't act. A Sophia Loren lookalike, she would smile at the audience and point to her fellow actors on stage, nodding approvingly to indicate one of us had said something funny. Since in her mind the whole audience was there to watch her, she was confident that whatever she found funny they would too. She got straight into the Royal Shakespeare Company. I went to see her in *Much Ado*, nodding approvingly and pointing to Judy Dench. She spotted me in the audience and, I swear to God, from the stage waved at me and made the hand signal to call her.

I wanted to follow her there but first I needed to get rid of my Chicago accent. So I put tiny weights on my tongue to master the English accent (it was like a little gym in my mouth). I worked out like Sylvester Stallone in *Rocky* … 'many

men many men many men' ... 'Tiny tuna tiny tuna tiny tuna.'
I never quite got the accent, but I learnt to do things with my
tongue that very few can – this skill landed me a job at the
Royal Shakespeare Company.

Trevor Nunn told me he can remember seeing nothing like
my audition before – not that it was good, he had just never
seen anything like it.

For the next five years I played every slut, wench and milk-
maid: underpants on my head as a mop cap, squeezed into a
corset that brought my navel to my neck and breasts so high I
could wear them as earmuffs. There I was up on the RSC stage
speaking a kind of Elizabethan porno, holding my Bo Peep stick
'Err, you mustn't shaaaft me kyyynd Sir. Oyyym just a simple
buxom wench, I am. I may look it but oymm not a slut.' From
there I went on to play a whole range of non-speaking prosti-
tutes, competing with another upstart tart, Juliet Stevenson. We
tried to out-whore each other, spending hours in make-up to
see which one of us could cover ourselves with the most pox.
We had no lines but we would improvise as whores, in the back
of the set gossiping about who had what stuffed down his
codpiece and these rude people like Patrick Stewart would tell
us to shut up. We were having a conversation for God's sake
while he was blithering away 'acting' or whatever he called it.
Spitefully, we would do bigger and bigger whore acting behind
him, scratching our lice and pox and swaggering until he was

rendered invisible to the audience. That's why he had to go to the Starship Enterprise – to get away from us.

Harder than whore work was wimple work – try coming through a doorway without ripping your head off. Nun work was the easiest; I once brought a friend from the audience on stage under my habit and, to up the ante, he lit up a cigarette.

Then one day an innocent, well-behaved Juliet Stevenson and I were cast as nymphs in *The Tempest*. We had white and blue screaming banshee hair, hideous aquamarine chiffon flowing gowns and white faces. Not so much nymphs as Jewish women on a shopping spree. Each night we were lifted on an elevator that rose from the bowels of the stage and when we got on the stage we were usually in a state of hysteria from just looking at each other; a once dignified Michael Horden was heard mumbling to Alan Rickman, 'I'm so ashamed.'

When I had time off at Christmas and other holidays I had to go home – there was no choice. I received relentless letters pleading with me, reminding me I owed them these trips. When I wasn't dragged away to Evanston, my parents visited me, continuously. We used to call them the Scuds, as in missiles. When my parents came to town, the whole company would fight for seats at the house I shared with Alan Rickman, which we called 'Shakespeare's Sauna' as all the walls were pine. They almost went AWOL from their plays because what was going on at my house was far more theatrical.

When my mother would show up, fresh from the train station, she'd drop her bags and re-enter, sweeping with a broom and for an encore she'd drop to her knees and clean the corners of the room. The house was a sell-out. The sofas over-flowed with younger versions of Jonathan Pryce, Zoë Wanamaker, David Suchet, Ian Charleson and others, all waiting with bated breath. Then my father would enter in a Swiss Alpine hat with feather, tweed jacket and cigar jutting out of his mouth, firing rapid machine-gun insults at me. After particularly vicious one-liners, the audience would erupt in applause.

Both parents working as synchronised killers, who kept mentioning how crazy the Royal Shakespeare Company must be to let me join, my father playing up to the crowds: 'Well, they must be going down the drain, for them to take her.' My mother would harmonise with, 'I think the theatre is after her money.' She always thought I had to pay people to befriend me. When I was still at drama school in Glasgow, I remember my mother panicking on the phone. 'Who is this Clydesdale Hillhead and where does he come from?' She thought I was paying some man with personal cheques to be my boyfriend; she had found the stubs.

I said, 'Mom, Clydesdale is my bank in Scotland. And the branch is in Hillhead.'

So when I got into the RSC, they thought I'd slipped someone bribe money. I told my father, I was actually being paid £72

95

a week and he responded, 'Oh, that's why they took you. Who else would work for nothing?' After the shows he used to snarl at me, 'Whoever you're playing, you're always Ruby Wax.' I couldn't argue with that. He used to take Rickman aside and ask him seriously how many people were laughing at me and how big a fool was I making out of myself. 'Come on, you and I know she's a sad sack and a kook.' Alan would respond, 'No, actually Mr Wax she's very talented.' And my father would come back with, 'What do you know, you're a Communist.'

Once after a show my dad came to Jane Lapotaire's birthday dinner at the Dirty Duck pub where he insisted on paying for everybody. The company who were well established actors by then said, 'Oh no, Mr Wax you don't have pay for us.' And he replied with a derogatory smirk, 'But I do. You're all Ruby's little friends. When you're famous, you can pay for me.' Michael Horden piped up, in a sad voice, 'But I am famous.' My father just slapped him on the back, sneaked a fiver into his hand and said, 'Yeah, sure, old man.'

Years later, I was being interviewed on TV. The other guest on the Gloria Hunniford Show was Michael Horden, who was by now Sir Michael. My father happened to be in the green room. I saw Michael after my interview, looking really shaken, he said, 'I've just met your father again and I said "Remember me?" Your father said, "No," slapped me on the back and gave me another five pound note.'

Later my father lectured me on how tragic it was that somebody that old had to do something so disgraceful for a living and did I want to end up like that?

While I was still at Stratford, I complained to Alan Rickman about my frustrations at having to play whores and nuns. Not even 'whore one', 'nun one', but 'whore three', 'nun six'. It wasn't good. I was meant for better things and I started getting suspicious that I couldn't act. He suggested I write my own shows and he would direct them, saying if I wrote like I talked, I'd have a future. I wrote like a possessed woman and eventually handed him this pile of mayhem, which he miraculously wove into a show. Even though I couldn't spell, I could write. I'd spew out my lines or, as he described, would 'vomit' my rantings and he'd turn them into gold dust. When Alan said my lines I would become hysterical, no one does comedy like him.

The only problem was in all my shows I imitated Alan ... badly. He was always better at my stuff than I was. In the beginning, I wrote for myself and another whore/nun, Darlene Johnson, who was as crazy as I was, on stage and off. We began a season called *The Johnson–Wax Floorshow*, a surrealistic collection of sketches, presented in Darlene's squalid bedsit. In one I played Jesus who ran a Laundromat; in another Darlene played a catatonic who part-timed as an ashtray – you get the idea. We invited Trevor Nunn and the rest of the company, charging them 50p for a playbill, which was actually a dry-cleaner's pamphlet with our names penned over it. The rather large audience squeezed into her bedroom. We'd then enter behind a blanket, which we'd drop when we hit the middle of the floor and so the show would begin. Rickman directed from the sidelines.

I expanded my cast and the bedsit got too small. I wrote parts for (my prior audience) Jane Lapotaire, Zoë Wanamaker, David Suchet, Paola Dionisotti, Ian Charleson, Jonathan Pryce, Carmen DuSautoy, Richard Griffiths and moved to the RSC stage, still directed by Rickman, no longer on the sidelines but always finding the most theatrical and funny spin on an idea. One of the shows, *Desperately Yours*, starring myself (of course), Juliet Stevenson and Paola Dionisotti, transferred to New York. The other two actors had to be recast with locals. I said I could direct the show but after the American cast threatened to quit from my abuse, we had to send for Rickman to soothe and direct the badly shaken actors. They told me I used to mouth their lines as they spoke them, looking furious, as if they were killing the comedy – the little dictator.

The off-Broadway production was successful and when I called my mother to ask when she was coming she said with all the charm of Cruella DeVille, 'I vait for the reviews.' Thinking about it, it was better she didn't come as the play was partly about her. Agents and producers crawled out like lice to sniff my talent; they lunched me and flattered me and said, 'Come to live in America where we'll take your insides out and freeze-dry them, and we might even give you some money for it.' I swallowed their hype whole and I caught the disease of vanity. I thought 'Yeah, I must be a genius I'm going to take this bundle of talent to America and make moola.' Tragically, this was to be my undoing – where the world finally said a big 'Fuck off' to me.

I figured now was the time to hit LA. I was under thirty so I could still be considered 'fresh meat' and I knew I should go before I rotted, before gravity sucked away my perkiness.

On my arrival the omens weren't good – of all the thousands of cabs why do I always get in the one with the guy who's foaming at the mouth? I was obviously interrupting a running argument he was having with himself. Schizophrenics are always so self-centred, Me, Me, Me, it's always aliens living in their back molars, never anyone else's. I screamed, 'Yeah, we're all being invaded, buddy, not just you.' Finally, around midnight we pulled up in front of a scary gigantic hacienda that glowed banana yellow in the dark. This was to be my new home, which was arranged through a friend of a friend from London (now no longer a friend).

I was greeted by a woman in a white flowing nightie. She wore matching white powder around her nostrils and spoke a strange language, a combo of Spanish on helium and tongues.

Whatever smile I had on that night was smeared off when I entered my new abode. Demonic and decadent, the dark walls were covered with peeling paintings of Queen Victoria. My bedroom, a boudoir of wrought iron, was filled with something resembling rusted gynaecological instruments. Why lay out a hairbrush on a doily, when you can provide your guests with an old kidney clamper? The bathroom was a glass dome, a delight when you were sitting on the toilet and could look out over LA. The only problem being, all of LA could look back at you.

My first night there, a coke-induced satanic ritual was going on downstairs, the cast of *The Night of the Living Dead* were roller-blading around the house while 'mein hostess' screamed up at me, 'Come on down, they all want to meet you.' (Meaning they were short an orifice.) I locked myself in the bedroom.

My first day, I drove along Sunset Boulevard blinded by the sunlit sushi bars, salad bars, bar bars and Eurotrash boutiques. Even the palm trees seemed to be giving me the finger. I went straight to Rodeo Drive and noticed something seemed to be missing. What was it? Later I realised – it was life. I also noticed I wasn't dressed for the occasion: I was still fat so clothes never brought out the best in me. I went straight into an empty boutique and bought my white 'n' cream 'business gal on the go' outfit, size 14. This was to create the illusion that if I wasn't busy at least my outfit was. To this day I keep it enshrined in a bag in my closet as a symbolic reminder of how far I could wander from the gates of my own sanity.

I eventually moved into another home and what a home – I was hitting a vein where everything I touched was toxic. I moved into the Helen Twelvetrees Estate, aptly named after a starlet who was brutally murdered.

It was a crumbling mansion built sideways on a cliff, so scenery was always on a tilt. Due to a landslide, our pool gradually filled up with the house next door. The inmates consisted of Becky, a 40-year-old flower child who lived on a mattress, surrounded by kitty litter. She would come home from being raped by knifepoint and ask if this was normal for a first date. Head of the household looked like a 30-stone axe-murderer who I'm sure was making hard porn in the basement but said he had a deal with Universal. He'd come into the kitchen looking like the *QE2* docking, rip open the fridge and snort. He had a pale Christian wife with bite marks all over her body – I never asked. My favourite was Marvin Lieberman, undiscovered comedy writer genius who lived in the broom cupboard where you'd hear him guffawing to himself through the night at his own wit. If you'd ask him what was so funny, the next thing you'd hear would be the sound of 80 locks clanking shut in case you stole the comedy idea of a lifetime.

I had gone to LA full of the muse and was mentally gangbanged. It was like a cartoon when a cat happily skips after the mouse and suddenly – 'clang' – a giant hammer hits him on the head and he's squished to about an inch thin. That was how I finally left LA, squished and wobbling. I had aspirations to become an actress so I went on a round of auditions for TV shows. Your personality is wheedled away by the lure of the buck until you think, 'Yeah, a sitcom about a ditsy brunette who shares an apartment with a blonde dancing teacher, that's a great idea.' Those are the sitcoms they wanted, a ditsy brunette who lives with a dancing teacher. Ditsy, for those of you who don't know, means ugly friend of the blonde girl with pointed breasts. This following dialogue is a sampling of the scripts I was handed. As I acted it I felt like that donkey they force to jack-knife off the high dive. My part was Rona, the ditz.

RONA: Hey, big date tonight, Barbie?

BARBIE: Very hot date with that cute guy who lives next door. He's so cute. I hope he doesn't try and kiss me on the first date.

RONA: He can kiss me on the date or any other part of my anatomy.

BARBIE: Oh don't feel so bad, Rona, you're not so bad. Someday, you'll meet Mr Right.

RONA: I'm not looking for Mr Right. I'm looking for Mr Right Now.

BARBIE: (*Ding*) Oh, there he is. Don't wait up honey. And listen Rona don't worry, some day your prince will come.

RONA: Yeah, the only tongue I'm gonna get around here is in my TV dinner.

The audience titter sadly.

As I read for the part, tears would run down my face. Afterwards the casting people would wonder why I'd whoop with joy when I didn't get the role. It was at this point I said 'No' to acting and 'our lady of the white powder' from Hacienda Banana where I used to stay said she could fix me up with a bigwig scriptwriter who needed a partner. He read my work and liked it. Up the canyon I drove to meet David Lyons. When I arrived, I couldn't figure out how the house was hanging there, the back of the house was shoved into the mountain, but the front hung out over nothing but air as if saying 'fuck you' to gravity. Those LA canyons are piled high with those precarious hanging homes; they remind me of the Tower of Babel, each maniac trying to get closer and closer to heaven and further and further from their minds.

So David lived at the very peak of Coldwater Canyon (such a comforting name). There was even a hammock on a jutting piece of patio; which if you swung on, the only thing between your butt and 4,000 feet to the ground was the odd swooping hawk. I found him swinging on the Hammock to Hell and he reminded me of Hugh Hefner, father of the *Playboy* Empire, in his smoking jacket and manly tweed slippers. But instead of the pipe hanging out of his mouth, he had a joint. He invited me inside the ultra-modern house and I followed him gratefully as skydiving wasn't part of my repertoire. I crawled into the kitchen and secured myself on a bar stool that was more IUD than stool. It ended in a prong, which I assumed you were supposed to insert in your buttock.

A tiny, blonde elf emerged from the bedroom, which he introduced as his fiancée. Dora, he assured me was very intelligent; I was just frightened she was going to bite my ankle. I always wonder why men find these miniature, foetus-sized blondes so enchanting because by my calculations if the man was lying on top of her: (a) he would kill her, (b) she would span the length of a pair of his underpants. To me it would be like having sex with a bread roll. Dora was dismissed to make something Japanese in the kitchen; I was told they only ate Japanese things. Anyway, David told me he was feeling very centred and so launched into the story of his masterpiece, which he wanted me to work on with him, 'Spiderella'. Dora returned to toss him some raw fish and he regurgitated the plot, which I found completely compelling:

Once upon a time there was a big B-movie star, the queen of tacky horror films, called Bella. Like everyone else in Hollywood she wants to look young forever. So she goes for weekly injections to a strange crypt/beauty salon. The resident German doctor believes he's discovered some age-delaying serum. The stuff he uses is squeezed from the sack of some rare South American spider. (Note: this is twenty years before any of us heard of botox.) Also, I don't know the technical name for when a man is attracted to a spider, but he has got the hots for the bug. (Note: these ideas are flowing from the mind of a man who is sleeping with a five-inch woman, so it makes sense.)

We know something has gone terribly wrong with the serum when Bella is in the toilet of Le Bistro on Rodeo Drive and we see from under her cubicle eight life-sized spider legs sprouting. Now we're in a Jekyll and Hyde situation – when it really isn't convenient, Bella will turn into a human-sized spider. Her personality changes with the transformation. In real life she's a demure Southern belle; when she's Spider Woman she becomes a deadly femme fatale filled with lust, vanity, gluttony, avarice – the stuff that's beneath most of us when you scratch the surface. After a particularly dramatic transformation, where she webs up Rodeo Drive, causing disastrous traffic jams, the Mayor of Beverly Hills calls upon the world's most famous Exterminator, Buck. And this is where the love story begins.

Our hero, Buck (think Rhett Butler), tracks down this destructive pest. When he meets Bella, he believes she's in danger as the monster's trail drew him to her home. They fall in love and they get married after the doctor tells Bella he's found the antidote, so we are lulled into believing it's all going to end happily. But on the honeymoon bed, we suddenly see a spider limb wrap around Buck's neck. As the legs spout around him and Bella scampers out the window, he assumes it's the lethal spider who is carrying away his loved one. A chase begins up and down the buildings of Beverly Hills, ending at Bella's favourite haunt, the top of the Beverly Hills Town Hall. Trapped in Buck's nets, she confesses that not only is she his wife, but she's the spider. There is no cure. A distraught Buck allows her to give him the lethal bite and the last shot is of them both, transformed into eight-legged spiders, making love on top of the now web-infested Hollywood sign.

I thought this was a brilliant idea and spent the next year and two months driving up to Valhalla to his hanging house and eating raw fish. We would sit in a darkened room, ten hours a day, in front of the glowing computer while he shrieked with laughter at my lines, telling me I was brilliant and this script would win me riches and that when the screenplay was finished all of Hollywood would be on their knees to me. Each night I left drained but confident. I would return to my haunted house smirking at what a comedy genius I was and run into Marvin who also believed he was working on the next Oscar winner. Over the kitchen table we tried to outsmirk each other – it was a showdown of smirks.

Throughout the time I worked on this script my father came to see me about a hundred times. Each time he would forbid me to work with David, giving me, 'I'm your father, you can't give me a minute of your time? You don't have to waste your life working on this, you have money and this is going to get you nowhere.' Thank God I had the sense never to tell him about the plot of the film.

When I wrote the last line David called his agent from William Morris and insisted he drive up the mountain because he said the script was 'too hot' to drive down the mountain. As the agent read it I watched him, panting with excitement, expecting at any moment he would throw down the script and say, 'Let me kiss you with my tongue.' I waited four hours and then the agent put down the script and said, 'I don't get it.' That was the last time I saw David. I swore life would never disappoint me like that again. I imagine the film was never made because I never saw it in the movie theatres – end of story.

Months later I tried to write another script but I was too depressed and the more depressed I got, the worse my writing became. Eventually it was down to:

'Hello, how are you?'

'Fine.'

'Would you like to come in my house?'

'No.'

'OK.'

I was empty – the great lines had flown.

Eventually I had a nervous breakdown. I hated the weather, fucking bright and sunny – happy fucking weather. Every fucker roller-skating and eating frozen fucking yoghurt and having a nice fucking day. I hated every smiley face. I hated every confident fucking grinning waiter who told you about his fucking Fish of the Day and launched into a speech about his acting classes, like that would lead anywhere. I would think, *Sweetheart the only hole that's gonna make you any cash ain't your mouth*, but they seemed oblivious to failure, so confident they would make it. I hated those people because they reminded me of me – the me who went to England thinking, 'Yeah, sure, I'm getting in the RSC,' just as cocky as them. But I saw myself superior because now I had scored a dose of depression. Was there ever anyone who was depressed who was an idiot? No one. Van Gogh, Sartre, Nietzsche, Beethoven and now me. All brilliant.

Some jerkoff referred me to Dr Aaronson, psychiatrist extraordinaire. He told me I should get to know myself while he slipped out to get a corn beef sandwich. I didn't understand his request. He told me to meet myself on a road and have a conversation. I came up with:

'Hello, hello, how are you?'

'I'm fine.'

'Who's talking?'

'Me.'

'Who's me?'

'You.'

'Why?'

'Because we're nuts.'

Things were bad but they got worse. One day I had a brainstorm and decided I'd work as a volunteer with insane people so that I could be with folks like me but I couldn't settle on which particular mental disorder I should work with. Day after day I'd drive to a different institution, fill out the forms and never return. My last application was to the UCLA Hospital, Psychiatric Unit, working with disturbed kids. I lied at the interview, claiming I'd done a lot of improvisational work with troubled children in London; amazingly they believed me and offered me the job.

On my first and only day, I told all the kids to make up a scene and present it to me. They all seemed to like the idea so much that I left the room to smoke and let them get on with it. When I came back, they were all gone – the window was open. Do I need to tell you I was fired?

My final port of call en route to Insanity was at the Beverly Hills night school, where I enrolled in a six-week shorthand course. My idea was to get a job as a film studio secretary and work my way up to chairmen of the board. After six weeks, we were tested on our shorthand skills, the teacher rang a starting bell and I applied my sharpened pencil to paper. Later, I was summoned to the office and the teacher asked nervously if something was wrong at home. I looked blank and she passed me my test paper. It was covered with loops, nothing but loops. I had sat there in class for six weeks, completely out of my mind, imagining I was learning to write shorthand and not taking in anything. This was the summation of my knowledge – loops.

I was told by a specialist I had a disease called Epstein Barre. I lay in bed for two months; so weak I couldn't move, turned the colour of Gouda cheese and was so crazy I started to think that *Love Boat* was an excellent show.

Then one day, one of the Monkees, Mickey Dolenz as in 'Hey Hey we're the Monkees ...', called me and offered me a job back in England writing a TV show. He said it was sardonic, vicious and dark; it was right up my alley. I jumped out of bed, scampered across the carpet to the mirror and stared at myself. The yellow, which had been there for months, faded from my face and I watched as the blood returned.

6

FAME

ENDLESS ARTICLES ON HEALTH will yabber on, telling you stress is caused by longer hours, more traffic, bad meat, but I'll tell you one thing that really pumps up the dissatisfaction bubble without you even realising it – envy. Here's a simple test to see how much envy you're carrying: open the pages of *Hello!*

Are you happy for those smiling celebrities, living in perfect homes, with their perfect partners? Or do you some-where, secretly in you bowels, wish they and their perfect spawn would be run over by a stampede of buffalo? When you browse through *Tatler* and see Baroness Von Fronkestien de .

al Flaezziti, laughing with some coke-infused viscount, does your bile rise? Do you think, why her and not me? Worry no more, these are normal reactions. When someone achieves fame and soars up into the celebrity heavens, it's the natural order of things that the underlings won't abide it – nature abhors someone who flies above the rest of the flock. So like in Greek tragedies, when someone gets too big for their boots, or sails too close to the sun, that special person is hit by a lightning bolt to balance things out. That's called Divine Justice. It's just God's way of saying, 'No way José, get down here.' (*Ruby Wax.*)

I'm filled to the brim with envy and do you know who really pisses me off the most? Models. You see, I'm in touch with my feelings of yearning and fury. What a life! What they do for a living is walk up and down a plank. That's it. Oh, and pivot and for this they're paid $10,000 a day. For $10,000 I'd sell a kidney. They pivot. If I had the length, believe me, I'd be up there. Oh, PS on top of the non-job description, most men want to sleep with them.

I once had to review the haute couture fashion shows, so they flew me to Paris. Sexy music starts and stick insects begin to parade down a plank, cheekbones on stilettos. All newborns, why not just toss a foetus down a runway? And the colour of these people? They are tawny, that is their flesh tone. Everywhere you look, tawny, tawny, tawny. I have to buy this colour, they grow it. Long legs take hours to rotate around those hard jutting hips and then they see something on the ceiling that makes them incredibly angry and then they pivot. Next they strut 'n' pout at you again, wearing antlers, roller blades, wimples, moose heads, jumbo jets, pizzas – things you can really use in your life.

Then the male models come out, following the female sticks, laughing like they're lads, larking about, skipping, wiggling, shaking themselves, flicking towels at each other and we're supposed to believe they're not homosexuals at all. Taking off a jacket and flinging it on again. They're having the time of their lives and you scum will never know what it is they're laughing about. But you chuckle to yourself because you know, but they don't, that by the time they're 40, they'll be melted down and made into glue.

At the end of the show the designers come out to take a bow. Do you know what they look like? Have you seen Tommy Hellfinger? To me he looks like a pickled coconut head in a 500 mile an hour g-force wind. If you put a fish-hook in someone's cheeks and then reeled them in, if they were a 71-year-old halibut, they would look like him. Dare I mention Valentino here? A hovercraft of hair comes out, with a small man underneath – this is Valentino, so bronzed it looks like he's wearing George Hamilton's skin. The audience is packed with Eurobitches preserved in formaldehyde.

Rich, mean, bitchy divas, with eyes tight, tight, tight, like
bulging lizard eyes – I kept expecting the tongue to flick out
and catch a bug. A 2,000 year old facelift next to me put her
crab claw on my lap and kept opening and closing it. I realised
she wanted me to pick up her programme off the floor, because
if she bent over, she'd rip her forehead off. I also met Karl
Lagerfeld. He does not look like a well man. He puts white
powder on his head, white powder, like his skull was sniffing
cocaine. I can't say there was much hair. Maybe he took one
hair from his nostril and one from his chin and tied it back in a
ponytail. Clearly, I'm not going to be asked to model so I don't
mind that I've burnt my bridges. But I feel better for spewing
my feelings. So much better not to carry too full a tank of envy.

Anyway back to my life ...

Having had my ego butchered, burnt and served up cold,
it was time to return to England. After the TV show I wrote
for Mickey Dolenz, which I wasn't in, I started to write and
perform my own comedy. It was more out of the need for
catharsis than anything else. I wrote very anti-American material, which made me feel like a tattletale child rebelling against
the bully. America mowed me under when I was a child, and it
mowed me under now. I failed there, twice, it had kicked my
ass out of its bosom. I also started writing for *Not the Nine
o'Clock News* where my speciality was virulent anti-American
sketches. From London, my father's so-called friends sent him

articles quoting my material. He was furious, writing daily, 'How dare you criticise your country, the greatest country in the vorld, where every day millions of Mexican's swim over the border, wire clippers clamped in their teeth to snip their vay to freedom, for a chance to come and vash your underwear. If you hate your country so much you should move to Russia where they stick you up against a vall and shoot you.' (Which I think he wanted to do to me.)

In the letters I could taste his fury, as the writing got smaller and smaller and more jaggedy, until the end where his signature was so tight and scratchy, it looked like an angry bird dropping, like the sign of 'Zorro'.

He particularly hated one piece where I pontificated on the history of the American 'go for it' spirit. I wrote:

We needed that 'gung-ho spirit' when we first came to our shores, wearing those ridiculous costumes with the buckles on our hats. We needed to feel the 'go for it' spirit to conquer a country full of wild turkeys and people whose only vocabulary was 'ugh'. That very spirit made us move across the country like an army of termites. A teeny weenie army of termites carrying itsy bitsy Gucci accessories. And after hundreds of years of termite work, we put up that Statue of Liberty with a bowel full of tourists and a head full of pigeon pee. And we opened our arms to all people of the world and said, 'Come, come to our shores.' We opened our arms to spics, wops, gooks, and said, 'Come, come and clean our homes, come and mow our lawns.' We opened our arms to the Negro people and said, 'Come, come you can be a winner just like us. We were just kidding about the picking cotton, it was a joke. Anyway you got a couple of nice tunes out of it.' We said to these people, 'You too can be a winner, especially if you sing like Aretha Franklin or have a gold medal around your neck.' We said, 'Come on everybody, drink a Coke and be a winner.' And that's what America's all about. Either you're a winner or you're the other half of the population walking around the streets of New York with your genitals hanging out, drinking five star petrol and barking at pigeons. That's the only clue that we might have got it wrong.

This kind of stuff made my father really mad.

And this very work that outraged my father to the point of an ulcer landed me my first television show, called *Girls on Top* which I wrote and co-starred in with Dawn French and Jennifer Saunders. While we worked on the scripts in my tiny one-room flat, it never occurred to me that it would eventually go on the air. Even when we acted in it with Tracy Ullman and Joan Greenwood, it was like we were having a party in an insane asylum. So when it finally was on television for public consumption, I was surprised to find people I'd never met smiling at me in the streets.

I was playing someone 'kooky' in the show and I was applauded for it. My father assumed this very trait was something to be deplored, to be ashamed of. Mommy and Daddy never approved of me, but now I had strangers who did. Men used to walk past me as if I was invisible; now they stared. What was the difference why they stared? They stared. And if you crossed your eyes and shut off your brain, you could pretend it was because of a desire for you. If you'd been ignored in the playground, my God is that revenge! Now you're prom queen and you didn't even have to shave your legs. And then I started to think 'Yeah, maybe I am really something special.' And that's exactly when I lost the plot. Because fame can 'seriously damage your health'.

Let me not get too hard on the subject, there are fantastic perks to fame; the main course may kill you, but the side dishes are good. When you want to get a table at a restaurant or your hair done and you realise if you mention your own name that the puckered anus on the end of the phone will start to ease up and the love juice will flow. When you get, 'Oh, yes, Miss Wax, we can get you a table in three minutes', something in your heart does give a leap. Or when you board a plane and some homosexual steward insists on upgrading you and carries you into first class as he handfeeds you nuts, this is good.

But the curse of it is, you start to expect this high-octane attention, this adoration and one fine day, when it doesn't come, the agonising, cold turkey will. Believe me, I had my own withdrawal experience many times. Once returning from America, I asked for my upgrade which, as I said, I'd gotten very used to. The woman at the counter said, 'And who the hell are you?' I was beside myself with rage, steaming with self-importance and proceeded to try and list my credits, but all that could come from my lips was, 'I'll have you know I work in a public field.' Like I was some kind of professional heifer. I was a cow, I couldn't describe myself any better. The woman just sneered and who could blame her.

Fame fit my particular neurosis like a glove. I craved attention due to lack of it in early life and now I hit a gusher. I understood I was using fame in the same way you'd use a bandage to cover up a tumour. The real festering neediness was still below the surface, though on the outside I smelled of success. Fame delayed my visit to the Priory by about ten years because of this delusion that if the public think you're OK – you're really OK. But I must have had an inkling something was wrong, because I became fascinated with observing how people behave when they've caught the disease of fame.

In the name of self-knowledge, I convinced the BBC to let me do a series on famous people. I wasn't interested in the least where the famous person shopped or who they screwed,

The happy workers at the casing factory (see page 10).

Barbara, my father's secretary, in full wig with Robert, his vice-president.

The Wiener wagon – my father's mode of transport (see page 34).

'Hello, blue eyes' (see page 30).

President of the Horse Club and due-paying member (see page 35).

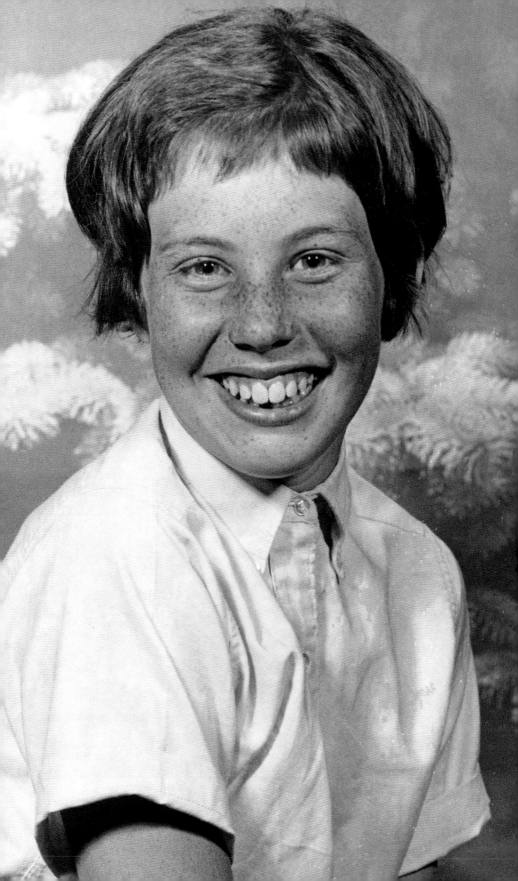

Camp Agawak; as a happy camper specialising in warfare (see page 44).

The golden couple.

Battle of the snowstorms: sharing her inner joy with her family (see page 32).

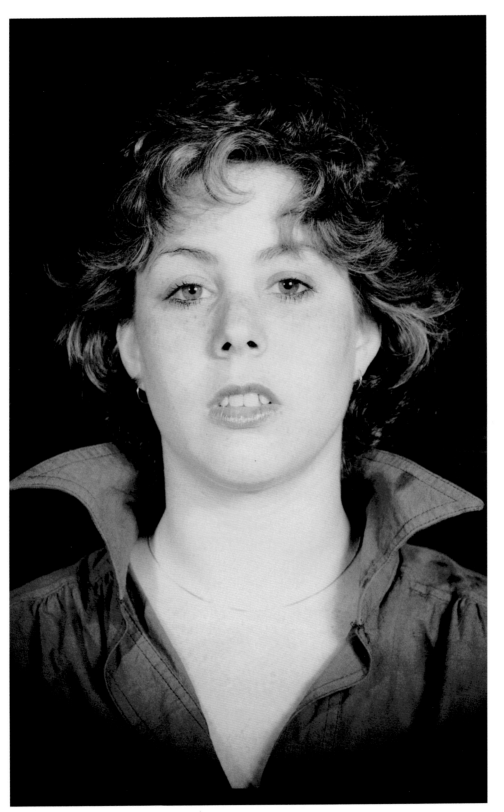

The disturbed teenager... darkness enters.

Graduating as (almost) the most popular girl in the class.

instead I asked questions that would help me understand them and therefore myself. I wanted to see exactly who they really were behind the mask, what had happened in their lives to make them want to wear it, and how wearing the mask affected them. I know that my interviewees were in another galaxy, they were 'Big Mother Superstars', the kind when they walk down a street, people drop to their knees and point, 'Oh, my God it's her!' and I have a teeny TV show on this sliver in the sea called England and am very well known at my dry-cleaners. But to be able to get close and observe these behemoths helped me understand the psychology of fame and the need for it.

Why we go for fame in the first place

People will go to any length to compensate for lack of attention at home.

Eddie Izzard once told me he used his audience to nurture him and compensate him for the loss of his mother who died when he was very young. He would jump through whatever mental hoops he had to to get audience approval, confessing to them his biggest fears and if at the end of a show they still approved, it felt similar to a mother's unconditional love. Same heat.

Most of the other famous people I've interviewed never feel satisfied. Fame cannot compensate for what you lack inside. Nothing can fill a hole because the human being does-n't have any gauge to know when it's full. A dog will only eat till it throws up. Human beings keep on going till they end up in rehab and beyond because, as wonderful as the first hit of VIP-ness is, you'll endlessly be chasing for more and more hits.

It's so like cocaine: you have to keep upping the dose. This is also because for some reason we can't sustain feelings of pleasure. If we could, I wouldn't be writing this; I'd be satis-fied with all my earlier works.

When you get a hit of attention it never really feels that good because somewhere down below you know you don't deserve being treated in this 'special' way and you'll eventually bust yourself for thinking you're above the rest. One day a little voice will whisper in your ear, 'Who the hell do you think you are, to demand so much?' It's a horrible thing called hubris – it's the ego police.

The human being wasn't meant to be adored by a public, they were meant to be human; to shop, eat, sleep etc. But to suck attention from others is not part of our existence manual and eventually leads to distress and breakdown. Why no one writes a gigantic billboard that reads 'Outside attention can seriously damage your health' I do not know.

Our prisons are other people's eyes; our cages are their thoughts.

And the thicker the armour, when the star begins to take

their myth seriously, the harder it is for the real person underneath ever to come out and play again. They've mummified
themselves like those rare butterflies, pinned for all to view. It's
The Night of the Living Dead because they can't relate to
anyone normal again. So now they have to find other freaks to
surround themselves with because they don't even breathe the
same air as Mr Average. My question is: how can they still be
an artist when they become the observed rather than the
observer? Because surely the very job of the artist is to interpret real life to the masses, to hold it up for us all to see in a
clear light. If their eyes are turned inward, what is the public
looking at?

Another symptom of the illness is that you start lashing out
at people around you who believe that you are 'special', who
place you above them. A hatred forms towards the groveller.
This is another strange kink in human behaviour. When someone is given adoration, the adored one acquiesces by taking the
whip and beating the shit out of the victim. Why is this? Why
do we ultimately punish those who offer us power? You see
those little fearful faces looking up and rather than be grateful
that they think you're wonderful, you want to smack them,
hard, on the head. I've often used the technique of treating
stars like normal people (a form of torment to some of them).
My way of helping to relieve them of their burden is to try and
deflate them and I know that somewhere under their armour

they're saying, 'Thanks, I couldn't stand being me for one more second.'

I used this deflating technique when I first interviewed Rosanne. She liked me because I sort of busted her. At one point we were lying in her empty bathtub, as you do, and she was yabbering on about how she wanted everything her way. I said, 'That's because you're just a big pig.' After a long silence, she started to laugh, she called me a pig back – which I am.

I could really see who Rosanne was under the mountain of crap fame brought her, a naturally brilliant comedian who had the gift of laughing at her lot in life, which was as appalling as it gets. She told me a story about when she was a young wait-ress at the lowest of the low fast-food chains called 'Chuckie Chicken'. There she met the first guy she ever liked who liked her back. She shared her feelings with another waitress who bluntly told her that the man of her dreams was a pervert: alone in the kitchen he used to take the frozen chickens from the deep freeze, wank into their headless neckholes and then throw them onto the fryer. Rosanne thought of this with a mixture of hilarity and pain, just as she did the rest of her trailer-trash past, but nothing was as depressing and degrading as the million-dollar lawsuits, the hangers on and the husbands who tried to exploit and use her.

Another problem with fame is no one hears the clock tick-ing as loudly as the beautiful. Have you ever noticed, on the big silver screen, you rarely see someone who was beautiful once, getting older? I will tell you why – because it's an unconscious reminder that we are all going to die. You hear the public say with distain, 'Oh, did you see what she looked like?' avoiding looking in the mirrors themselves. That's why the dead stars are loved so much, they can never change – of course, they are changing in the coffin where they lie but that's way too off the planet to think about (I do all the time). There are exceptions, when we see an old star rise again, but the talent has to be so enormous it deflects from the cracks of time and if their talent shines, the audience think to themselves, 'How brave they are to show up in that condition' and 'How resilient they are that they aren't dead yet'. If they are bad actors they get, 'Didn't she look like shit?'

There is no peace for the beautiful. I remember finding Sharon Stone in her dressing gown with her make-up girl. She pointed in horror to the new crease on her knee. She said she felt the clock ticking constantly, and this was just another early warning sign.

I couldn't crack Madonna. I couldn't see who she was under the mask. The persona was too hard and she was surrounded by too many people to ensure her real self would never come out again. I had to fly to Paris for the interview and we were lying on her bed at the Ritz, hordes of ass-wipes surrounding us, trying to act like she wasn't Madonna. One of them kept calling her 'Madge' and blushing at his own audacity. Everyone was in that hyperdrive they get around the famous, aroused, in a flop sweat, trying to out-funny each other. Do the famous pull that energy or do we just give it to them because we know they're famous?

To be honest, I also go into overdrive around them. I hate myself for this but it's true; the feeling being, if they like me, I must really be someone special, I must matter in the world, I have transcended my usual schmuckhood. When I'm with famous people I find myself verbally tap-dancing to please them, then I go home and slap myself for doing it. Most of the interviews I did were in this vein: the unpopular, warthog, tusked little girl was now with the most popular person on earth.

The whole time I was with Madonna I don't think she was really aware of me, only in how the interview was being shot. We each had a cameraman, my guy just pointed the camera at me, her cameraman (hired by her team) was sweating about angles, lighting etc. Everyone around her was obsessed with how she was going to look.

I worked overtime trying to humour her and eventually lost my erection conversation-wise. I was so frazzled by then I didn't know who I was anymore, let alone who she was. And then, to make it worse, you get the rules from the nicotine-pumped PR who is paid £5,000 a week to tell you not to ask anything personal. 'Oh, yeah, like I'm going to talk about the weather?' Their job is to look like they're hassled even though they're doing nothing at all. So she tells me in a tone like I'm going up for criminal charges, 'No personal questions.' The interview was awful, but the interesting thing is I looked great on my camera (I always have a strong filter – it is a rule all must obey) and Madonna, for all the futzing around, didn't look so hot that day on hers. (Divine Justice.)

Another time I had to deal with a PR harridan was when I interviewed Bette Midler. If you dig below the surface of some of these people you find a serious mound of self-loathing. Being near the famous lifts them temporarily from the reality of their lowly selves. I completely understand this sensation as a I share it myself. So the frazzled Midler PR gives me, 'You have five minutes with her in the hotel room, don't ask anything personal and whatever you do, don't ask her to sing.' Three minutes in, Midler and I start laughing in her hotel room, so I ask her to come to Harvey Nichols to shop with me. When you get them laughing they usually drop the mask. The PR lost her tongue when the star said, 'We're leaving.' We go to the fish section on the fifth floor, where I perform an emergency caesarean on a cod. And on the escalator down she sings her latest song while I do her backup. Later, I told the PR that she didn't mention that I couldn't handle fish with Miss Midler.

Of all the celebrities I interviewed, only Pamela Anderson was having the time of her life with fame because she is blessed with hardly any personal ambition. When I asked what she wanted out of life she said simply, 'To be a great ho'', which, for those of you who don't know, means, in poor white trash talk, 'to be a great whore'. How refreshing is that?

God blessed her with a Rolls-Royce for a body and she was using it for all it was worth. Can you imagine having that epidermis wrapped around you? It would be like being a walking funfair with an amusement park down your front. I know she had children but where did she give birth to them? Through her kneecaps?

There's no stretch marks, no bulge, just taut, tight, juicy flesh. Naturally, I asked if I could be her body double for the day and to my delight she said 'yes'. For my show I put on a matching red swimsuit (had to do a lot of upper thigh shaving and cut myself many times, as these parts of me had not seen the light of day for many years) and went on to the beach. I assumed a cheesecake position as Pammy's stand-in, buttock high in the air, head in the sand. The director shouted through his megaphone, 'Umm, the person in the red bathing suit, you're doing a wonderful job, but could you please leave the beach, immediately.' I wobbled off the set, the object of fascination for the whole silicone-fuelled cast. I guess they had never seen surgical free flesh before; certainly they studied me like I was a dead sea-cow that had been washed ashore. The director, as a consolation prize, did let me scamper with the babes along the seafront for the end shot of *Baywatch* – but while the other girls were rock solid, I fell sideways and had to be rescued out of my own fat.

Hugh Hefner was the only other famous person I found having a good time with his fame. His empire peddles young flesh, so there's a steady stream of grade A babe on tap. His job and his hobby segue perfectly; he has made the pact with the devil and won. You know in the American Constitution it says we have the right to pursue happiness but no one ever does? Well, he does. When I asked him what kind of a pick-up line he used when hunting female, he said, 'Hello my name is Hugh Hefner.' He knows what they're after and has no delusions. He's free from the usual vanity and envy and because of this, the fact he's beyond the clutches of fame's laws, famous men are in awe of him. Jack, Leonardo, Mick, Warren, go to his parties and line up to mingle with the maestro. Hugh is truly a happy bunny.

While a normal person is equipped to deal with disappointment, the famous have gotten flabby from over-indulgence, and their downfalls seem tragic. They aren't prepared for human misfortune, such as ageing. This is why their demises are so tragic. As a bejewelled claw grabs your hand at some party and a shrivelled walnut head says, 'Remember me', your heart breaks for them.

And now we move into extreme fame. The Deep Waters. People that would do almost anything for worldwide attention. In a class of her own: Imelda Marcos. Starting as a simple chorus girl from the country she took a gargantuan *tour jette* to first lady of the Philippines. She had no doubt of her ascension since she told me the Virgin Mary spoke to her as a child and guided her to her husband, Ferdinand. I wonder if the Virgin Mary told her that some day her husband would steal 170 million from the country he ruled, or did Mary mention some day she would own 100,000 pairs of shoes, the price of one pair being the annual income of one family? She definitely believed she was blessed. On one occasion at a Catholic church in Manila, Imelda, or Meldie as she liked to be called, was carried over the heads of the throng, deigning to touch various children to heal them of their infirmities. Some children even asked me to touch 'n' heal since I was sitting next to Meldie.

Along with her belief in supernatural powers, she also believed she could sing. I asked her to give me a tune, but she refused until she was in full costume (her bridal gown) and accompanied by her personal pianist. Seventeen songs later, I was reeling from her performance, which included a very sincere version of 'Feelings' and 'Yesterday' (she was an irony-free zone). She told me she used to sing privately for Mao Tse Tung and he loved it. If that doesn't prove he was mad, nothing does.

The room was overstuffed with relics from the Marcos reign: the odd Picasso, the Rococo style furniture, wall-to-wall framed photos of some of her best friends including Gaddafi, Idi Amin, Arafat, Saddam Hussein, Nixon, George Hamilton, Liz Taylor … who were just 'wonderful people when you got to know them' and 'really a lot of fun'.

Like most movie stars she started out treating her interviewer (me) like dirt for being a mere mortal. Luckily, I knew this was coming so I borrowed £150,000 worth of jewellery from Theo Fennel so she would at least respect my rocks. Later, by accident, in her home, which was crumbling in decadence and decay, she spied an old copy of *Hello!* in her rubbish bin, and my photo happened to be on the front cover. She went from giving her lackeys darting eyes that said: 'Get her out of here', to full-throttle ass-kissing in one swift second. I was immediately taken to her breast because suddenly she realised I too was sprinkled in celebrity dust.

Originally, I was allocated fifteen minutes with Meldie and not a minute more but as soon as her eyes hit the cover of *Hello!* she decided to give me three whole days. Excited to be with someone else 'famous', she let me investigate her account books – they filled a whole room, like an Aladdin's Cave of 'cooked books'. I ecstatically leafed through page after page of luxury items: Harry Winston necklace: £15 million. Hope diamond: £145 million, you get the idea.

On day three she took me to Congress to witness her being sworn in as MP. Her own children were dumped unceremoniously out of the limo on the way. She insisted on holding my hand all the way to Parliament House. As we entered hand in hand, she shouted out, 'She was in *Hello!*' They are so crazy in the Philippines. I got a round of applause and the Mayor of Manila stopped the proceedings and bowed to me. Back home during the celebratory dinner, she fork-fed me chocolate cake, as I sat on her lap. Later she ran about gathering gifts for me and the kids, pearls, a dress covered in gold, embroidered shoes, presents for Ed ... then, smiling, she pointed to the attic like a proud mother. I gave her all the attention and admiration she wanted, and in the end I was rewarded when she let me climb the stairs to the treasure trove, filled with the next stash of shoes.

O.J. Simpson also loved and needed his fame at any cost. He tried to have my camera crew around him constantly, resulting in us being with him seventeen hours a day. It was years after his murder trial and clearly America's interest in him had waned so he needed to keep us interested. The first night we went for dinner we'd only just ordered aperitifs when he remarked that he usually didn't drink, because alcohol made him sexually excited and out of control. To whet my appetite further, he added apropos of nothing that he once worked with Elizabeth Montgomery in a TV film about the notorious

Lizzie Borden. He then proceeded to recite a poem about this infamous American murderess:

Lizzie Borden had an axe
Gave her mother 40 whacks
When she saw what she had done
She gave her father 41.

The next day during filming, he insisted we drive by Judge Ito's house in Brentwood, where he rolled down his window and shouted, 'Asshole'. Then he asked in a buoyant way if we wanted to drive by the house where Nicole was murdered. Around lunchtime, I phoned a few restaurants to make reservations. When the maître d' found out who was coming, he hung up. Ironically, we spent the day driving around in a white van.

All he talked about was the details of the trial. His logic was like twisted spaghetti and, as the hours passed, my mind got fried from confusion. But I went on high alert when he told me that he once went to the Scientologists because he thought he had special powers (see Imelda Marcos).

When he was a football player he believed he could control other players on the field with his mind. He reported that Ron Hubbard himself concluded that O.J. didn't need to become a scientologist because he was at the highest level a human can achieve; that he, O.J. Simpson, was at the level of Jesus Christ. If you didn't think he was deluded before this, surely you do now.

At the end of the long, tiring day, during which O.J. mentioned many times that I reminded him of Marcia Clark, O.J. was joking around and at about one o'clock in the morning pretended to stab me with a banana like Norman Bates in *Psycho*. The following day, his agent explained that O.J. 'is such a kidder' – he loves to imitate scenes from films. When I asked what film he was imitating the night before, he said, *Cats* ... I couldn't dream this answer up.

When I got to London, this same agent told me to leave a message on O.J.'s phone saying the film we shot of him was damaged, as an April Fool's joke. I did leave a message but I said that the agent had slept with O.J.'s sister. I hope neither one of them comes and kills me for this.

7

MARRIAGE

I WAS WORKING ON *Girls on Top*, a TV show in London, when I first got the inner call to multiply. It was very late in the day – in other words I was getting long in the tube, about 35-and-a-halfish – late enough for ya? It wasn't a call so much to breed, more that I started to think: who's going to help me go to the toilet when I'm 92? I looked around and saw I was only working with women and figured none of them would and then I noticed my male director. I thought to myself, I have the career, a flat, what am I missing here? And then I realised ... Oh, a husband. And there he was, cute, young, tall (I could

133

suddenly break the mould of 5,000 years of short Polish Jews in one fell swoop).

Once I focused on Ed, I upgraded myself quickly. I used to roll into rehearsals practically in my old pyjamas. Now at least once a week, I shaved my legs. (Always a sign that sex might be on the cards.) And every morning I applied mascara (a clear warning that the woman is in heat – the minute the ovum shouts, 'Get going boys we're making eggs' the hand automatically reaches for the mascara wand) and I don't quite know why, I started stuffing rubber inserts in my bra. Dawn French noticed the enlarged breasts immediately and one horrible day, wrenched them from deep in my bra to show Ed, in her infinite cruelty. Poor Ed looked terrified as I grabbed the implants out of her hands, ran out of the rehearsal rooms, down Edgware Road, and hunched down to dig a hole and bury them behind a tree. Cars were honking and waving as I covered the last of the rubber cups in dirt. I waved back at the passing cars, trying to pretend everything was normal. Then I strolled back into the rehearsal room.

At first I'd thought 'he's not my type', but as the days wore on, you know how normal things can suddenly appear beautiful. His eyes got so blue and suddenly I thought his jokes were brilliant. Only days before they had irritated me, now I thought the man's a genius. Why had I never noticed this before? Such is the magic of hormones.

All too soon it was the end of the series. At the final party crowded with crew, Ed was in a corner, necking with some blonde PA. Dawn strode over to them, like a mafia Don and told the girl to 'Get lost'. Jennifer pushed me at Ed and eventually we left the party together. Just as we departed I was instructed by Dawn and Jennifer to inform them the moment penetration occurred.

The next morning, I pretty much ripped Ed out of me mid-sex and ran down the hotel corridor, knocking on the girls' doors with the news.

I thought it best to marry Ed without informing him first. I asked my shrink if I should marry him. She responded with, 'What does Ed bring to you?' I said, 'Heat.' She knew that my life so far felt cold and barren, so she said, 'That's good enough for me, that should be good enough for you.'

I actually proposed to Ed in Florence in a romantic restaurant over pasta. I told him if he was interested in marrying me he should move quickly, there was a whole queue of men waiting. Ed went on eating. I continued that I could schedule the wedding for April but only if he said 'yes' now. I think he nodded – I'm not sure. I booked a register office in Richmond for April 1988. Halfway down the short aisle, I told him how old I was, but it was too late for him to bolt. The registrar looked like a C.S. Lewis woodland creature with little hairs sprouting from her upper lip. She married us as I laughed

hysterically for reasons I cannot remember. I signed the register 'Best Wishes Ruby Wax' because I forgot what I was doing
and lost control even more – it was attended by Ed's parents
and all our close friends.

My own parents did not attend because when I had called
them in Chicago to invite them, my mother said to let her
know when it was over, as it seemed too much trouble to come
over right then. A week later, when my father found out I was
already married, my mother told me that he almost killed her:
he had dreamt of the day I would wed and he'd take me down
the aisle. Now, out of spite, my mother made sure that he'd
missed it.

My parents had met Ed, on a prior visit to London, and
liked him. My father kept saying, 'He's a prince – what's wrong
with the guy?' They thought he was nuts to be interested in me.
Even though my father missed the wedding, he still had some
fatherly advice for the groom. He pulled Ed aside one day and
advised him, 'You don't beat her enough.' Ed said, 'I don't beat
her at all.' My father just shook his head incomprehensibly.

In contrast to me, Ed's parents were the stuff fairy tales are
made of. Maybe I married Ed partly for his parents. Priscilla,
the daughter of an admiral, grew up playing elephant polo in
India with the Mountbatten set and she was bred to be a
charmer. At Christmastime Ed's mother would wheel in a
turkey on a silver trolley. Inside the turkey would be a goose,

then a chicken which contained a guinea fowl which had a harmonica in its stomach. At the end she would grab the harmonica and play for us. After Christmas dinner Ed's father, Cliff, and Priscilla would always put on a show for us. One year it was called the 'History of Aviation'. They dressed like airplanes and buzzed around the house with the 'Battle of Britain' as background music; doing loop de loops and shooting each other out of the sky. (They had obviously been up for nights making costumes and rehearsing.)

One year I tried to reciprocate and made Ed do 'Good Ship Lollipop', lying under me in a pair of tights. The seasonal shows were cancelled after that and were never mentioned again.

Nothing, but nothing, was too much trouble for his parents. Scones came out of his mother day and night. She'd run up and fluff your pillow before your head hit it and would wait at the end of your bed with a cup of tea when you woke. Can you imagine me marrying into that? It reminded me of those Dickens stories when the orphan, after years of abuse, finally walks into the warm hearth of a happy home. Ed's father was a Royal Marine commando. His speciality was jungle warfare, which included unarmed combat. Whenever I'd try and ask about how many people he had killed with his bare hands, Cliff would reply in gentle baby talk and rhyming ditties, I'd get 'It was on the good ship Venus, By God you should have seen us ...' He was the professional warrior and yet my father, who never saw active duty, had the instinct of Goebbels.

When my parents phoned at Christmas, Ed's father, the Colonel, would move to the other side of the room and go strangely silent. They met a few times, the first was at our house in London. Ed's mother opened the front door to my mother sweeping the front steps. Mrs Bye gave a charming, 'So nice to meet you.' And my mother responded with the fact that I didn't have the right kind of broom. Not even a 'hello', just straight into broom talk. Mrs Bye tried to change the subject, but my mother would not stop talking about the new broom and when was I buying one?

On our first big family outing we went to a fancy restaurant for dinner, where my mother proceeded to draw a picture of the broom on the tablecloth, using her fork to make outlines. The two sets of parents never really engaged, though Mrs Bye tried to feign interest in brooms. On my mother's way back to the airport, she kept describing the broom, as if she had never said it before, from the window of the jet she was still signalling about broom size. As soon as she landed in Chicago she called me to ask if I bought the broom yet, then launched back into what it should look like. Between the description of bristle length and type of handle, she mentioned that my Aunt Hambourger had died – I asked her to slow down – did she just say my aunt had died? My mother, furious said, 'I vant to talk about the broom.' Stubbornly, I asked again if my aunt was dead. My mother retorted angrily, 'OK, back the clock up 24 hours. She's not dead. Now about the broom ...'

When Ed and I got married, we moved into my flat, which I had decorated to look like a modern nursery school. Furniture was like big Lego blocks painted Miami colours, fuchsia, turquoise and yellow. Just to be different, chairs, tables, desks, beds, had three legs instead of four, so everything was very shaky. The walls and ceiling were aqua so the whole effect was like living on the bottom of a swimming pool. Anyway, now swimming around in my home was a husband. I had scored.

I guess Ed wanted a break from the perfect woman, his mother. So he couldn't have wandered into a better minefield than me. He wanted a roller-coaster ride where you never knew what was around the next bend and he got it. It was a thrill a minute in the early days. Later, he couldn't take the sick-making heights but then neither could I.

After we got married, I didn't know how I was supposed to act. How should you act as a wife? God knows I had no role models. The only image I had of married life was the man is supposed to beat up the wife and she's supposed to nag as hard as she can and clean the floors. So, I thought back to my favourite childhood sitcom, *Bewitched*, and made Samantha my image of the perfect wife. The fact that she was a witch underneath I could identify with. Also, her mother was a really bitchy witch; that felt right too. So, I tried to imitate Samantha. When Ed came home from work, I'd go, 'Oh, hi honey, I made you a martini with an olive in it. You must be exhausted from all that work – here Poopies, let me give you your slippers. [I wasn't sure whether me or the dog were supposed to enter at that stage.] Hey, schuckums, I made you dinner, just the way you like it' and I did try to make dinner, once. I thought marriage was just a temporary thing, so I made dinner. After all this was the honeymoon phase when you're still shaving your pits before sex, when you're still waxing. Later in marriage you let yourself overgrow like a neglected bush forest. In the end you can hear jungle drums coming from your crotch region – the squawking of tiki birds.

And then it started to dawn on me – this was a permanent thing; I was a regular primetime player on the marriage show. Neighbours were taking my role of 'wife' seriously: little cards would plop through my letter box inviting Mr and Mrs Bye for drinks at 8:00. And I wanted to burst into their home waving a firearm and scream, 'I'm not Mrs Bye, I'm me.' Ed told me I was overreacting, they were just being friendly and then that 'we' thing started, where couples address themselves as 'we'. I'm not a 'we', I'm a 'me'. So we'd go over to the neighbours and find ourselves saying things like, 'We don't believe in UFO abductions' and they would answer with, 'We too.' Then you'd leave really early promising to invite the two of them over for drinkies at your house.

The night would arrive and I'd be in a blind panic. Jesus Christ, what finger foods are you supposed to serve neighbours? You can't just toss them fistfuls of nuts, you have to buy expensive things and then put them on toothpicks: Brie, prosciutto, anchovies, those onion balls, and in what order do they go? I would quickly try to find *Bewitched* on the television to see what Samantha would do but could only find *Buffy* who puts a stake in people's hearts – that I could relate to. After a successful evening of more 'we' talk they'd 'reciprocate' by inviting 'us' back to their house for dinner and you know where this leads? To the fucking 'thank you notes' for having you to dinner, 'Yeah, the food went down and came out of my ass with great success ... Thank you'. After two more years of them eating your food and you eating theirs the conversation pond has pretty much run dry, suddenly the neighbours, just to up the ante, throw down this ace: 'We're pregnant!' Then I remembered why I got married in the first place – so I just dumped the diaphragm and Ed became another victim of the oestrogen mafia.

Now that I had been dubbed Mrs Bye (though if anyone every calls me this I ignore them, thinking they're addressing Ed's mother) and become part of this new state called 'couple-dom', I became transfixed by this strange institution. What possesses you to find another lump of flesh, call it your own and settle down?

First of all, where did we get the idea that there's just one other person in the universe with whom you can form this perfect union and who will feed all of your needs? If I counted all my needs, I figure I'd need 459 men to satisfy them all – one to make me laugh, one who knows the correct mechanics of foreplay, one who's good at plumbing, one who makes a good daddy, one who holds my head over the toilet after a rough night, one who tells me I look great even when I look like shit, it all adds up to 459. Anyway, maybe that's just me.

What is the glue that holds two humans together after the sex dies down and you've told all your stories twice? What is there, really?

In the pursuit of scientific evidence I have stalked couples while on holiday, to study what they have in common. Ed was kind enough to give me surveillance equipment for my birthday five years ago, which enables me to listen into conversations at quite a wide range. It involves an inconspicuous baseball hat that conceals an antenna, an aerial, earphones and a long-range mike. I listen to fat couples, sporty couples, reading couples, dancing couples, card-playing couples and believe me folks, there's not a lot going on.

This leads me to conclude, these people are together so they have someone to look at while they're eating. Nobody wants to masticate alone. They're not talking, let alone laughing, but God bless them, they have someone to face while they chew.

What attracted them to each other in the first place? I know you won't agree but I think it's all down to a smell; it's dogs sniffing each other in a park, we just happened to be standing up and holding drinks, but it's the same thing. The reason no one talks about it is it's hard to put the word 'smell' in a song. You would never sell a CD with the lyrics, 'I Will Always Smell You'. Or 'Can't Buy Me Smell'. No one else will tell you this because they're trying to sell you books, poems, films and Valentine's Day cards. I know you think it's your heart where passion lies, but next time you're with the man of your dreams, stick a nose plug on and watch how aroused you get. You'll see I'm right.

Couples

Once you've found your 'other half' you'll find there are various identifiable combinations. I think that these days, because we have so little time, you should know precisely what you require in a husband, beforehand. Apply the same foresight and precision you do when ordering off a Chinese menu – here are some handy categories, plus potential hazards.

Delta Woman with Alpha Man

Inspired by such stories such as Sleeping Beauty, Cinderella and

Pretty Woman, this is the prototype many women who are lazy seek. She imagines she will have time to skip around the house all day eating chocolates, while he slaves away to bring her money. Yes, it is the ideal fairy-tale coupling but I have a warning to go with this match. The Alpha Man is used to buying and selling in a speedy turnaround way and at some point he will treat you in a similar fashion. Be aware: you are just another commodity to him. In a short while, you will be bought and sold like a dumped stock. *Remember*: just as soon as protruding parts start to droop you will be replaced by a firmer copy of you, this is guaranteed. So steal what you can from the joint account while those bits are still pointing upwards.

Special Note to the Delta Woman
There are only two types of Delta Female who have ever successfully captured the Alpha Male!

The Silent Beauty
Oriental women have perfected being the Silent Beauty over centuries, having learnt to keep their eyes lowered and months clamped shut. Their status is slightly above a Louis Vuitton briefcase or Rolex watch.

I've known some very powerful Alpha Males who found a Silent Beauty in the cast of *Cats*. Watch her in the show; now use her in the bedroom. It's like bringing home the ultimate souvenir. But these 'Cats' only last a few years. They start making a mess and meowing loudly about how they gave up their flourishing careers. They have to be replaced very quickly before they start moulting.

The bad news for the Silent Beauty is once the crow's feet etch across their crystalline faces, they suddenly find themselves silently removed. Some go quietly and some suddenly find a voice ... in court.

If you don't have the looks, your only other option as a Delta Woman is becoming his Social Empire Builder.

Social Empire Builder

This role is exhausting as it involves constantly prowling for who's in and who's out as seen in the pages of *Tatler*, then gabbling and ass-kissing their way to inviting that A-list person to dinner. Even I have been invited by these social uber-host-esses to their dinner table because they were short a comedian.

Here's what happens. The uber-hostess drags you into the dining room like some prehistoric lump of meat; a mother tyrannosaurus feeding its young. You're flung at the feet of the fatcat husband who sits at the head of the table, proudly scan-ning the various heads of entertainment, government, acade-mia, literature etc. He very rarely contributes to the conversa-tion, just chomps on a cigar. The Silent Beauties just have to sit there with eyes lowered and mouth shut. You have to do all the talking 'cause that's what you've been hauled in for. If the conversation halts, the cordon bleu steak is practically ripped out of your mouth.

I once found myself at the same dinner table as Princess Diana. An uber-hostess used her as bait and I wasn't going to miss this experience.

Everyone was tense from pretending things were normal, but the laughs were so high-pitched, dogs could hear them. The men attempted the most terrible mother-in-law jokes; the wives were in a flop sweat, as they meandered through unamusing stories.

There was a terrible silence and knowing in my fibres it was my turn to talk because my plate was in the process of being removed, I launched into a story about one of the first times Ed and I slept together. Once I started, I was on the train with no brakes – this is how it went:

'We were on holiday in a Milan hotel room and after a drunken night together, I woke up to find Ed, huddled in a corner, hands over his mouth, in that silent scream pose – you know the Munch painting? I followed his eyes and saw under my head there was this pool of something brown, then I lifted my back and there was more brown stuff and now, panicking, I lifted my bottom and there was this gigantic lake of brown – I couldn't breathe. Very gradually I noticed a tiny silver piece of paper and I realised I must have fallen asleep on the hotel complimentary chocolate, which had melted under my head and worked its way between my cheeks.'

OK, it wasn't that brilliant but Diana liked it and invited me to go upstairs with her where we ripped open all the closets of the hostess and tried on her clothes. So the story has a happy ending. I have to say I fell in love. Like a schoolgirl crush, I did anything to make her laugh. She did top me though – she asked if I knew Will Carling was now working for Disney? I said I hadn't heard that. She laughed and said he was working on a film called 'Poke-a-Highness'.

And let us not forget today's most popular combination and the one that really doesn't work:

The Alpha Woman with the Alpha Man

Here's my theory on it. Once the man was the hunter and the woman the gatherer. But now everyone has the chance to hunt. With both partners as hunters, marriage has become a 'negoti-ated deal', but still someone has to be the gatherer because if both parties are out there beating their chests, who the fuck is ever going to pick up the towel? In the past it was his mommy. So he expects the same service from you, be you president or policewoman. The only way that fucking towel is going to get off that floor is if we hire someone to pick it up. This is where most modern marriages are heading. I predict that in the next millennium, the family unit will be made up of lots of hired

help. So they'll be hunters (which are both of you) and professional towel-picker-uppers. You'll have a staff instead of a family
who will even grow to love you if you keep paying enough. A
whole, huge staff, singing around the Christmas tree.
Eventually the husband will become more and more redundant.

'Just leave the sperm at the door, my secretary will pick
it up.'

8

BABIES

'*You've got to love 'em ...*' Albert Camus

Everybody tells you childbirth is the most beautiful experience of womanhood, when you truly become one with the earth – the ebb and flow of the tides, your womb connecting deeply to Mother Nature. Do not listen to these people – it is fucking hell.

When I found out I was pregnant, I wasn't going to let it interfere with my schedule. I just thought my upper half could still work while my lower half made babies. Wrong! God shuts

149

you down in order to grow another life; all IQ seeps from your fibres, you cannot dam the departing flood of intelligence. Thoughts get scrambled like switching between radio stations so now all you get is static with the occasional headline making its way through: 'Must eat now!' 'Must eat more now!' Thought is cancelled; the body becomes an emergency station to make blood, bone and tissue.

When I was eight months pregnant, I was asked if I'd like to make a documentary in Russia. 'Sure why not?' I said. 'What would be the problem?' Obviously I was in full denial.

Russia was a hellhole. Glasnost had not officially kicked in, so all documentaries still had to be approved through bureaucratic channels. No way could you just show up and take your pick of the citizenry, the interviewees were assigned to you: the Prostitute, the Factory Worker, the Housewife etc. This is why all documentaries at that time had the same people in them. Since everyone knew that Russian bureaucracy was a nightmare, London friends told me I needed a 'fixer'. They put me in touch with Veruschka, a crazy Russian. Veruschka was about 50 with purple hair, black painted lips and nails; she looked like an ugly Morticia. She spoke a combination language, half Russian half English, neither of which could be understood.

Verusckha had a peculiar hobby, she collected AIDS victims. They had to live in her house, where she would nurse them, unsuccessfully. At their death, she would throw a wild orgiastic death festival. Anyway, Veruschka said she knew the Minister of Arts and could squeeze him for a permit but she would have to go with me to Moscow. She arranged the journey on Aeroflot (luckily for her I didn't check how many crashes that particular airline had chalked up).

The opening shot of the documentary is on the wheels of an Aeroflot taking off, with me aboard it. What it doesn't show is that I couldn't get my seatbelt around my stomach, so when the wheels lifted up, the broken springs in my seat jackknifed me backwards into the lap of the passenger behind me. It must have looked to my fellow passengers as if I was giving the man behind me an upside down blowjob.

After our arrival in Moscow Airport, Veruschka drove like a fucking blind bat to the National Hotel. She couldn't stay long because she had to minister to an English AIDS patient she had brought with her to Russia. I tried to picture it: a guy in the final spasms of dementia is pulled from his deathbed by an insane purple-headed person who informs him he needs to come to the sweltering heat of Russia to die. I wonder what passed through his mind?

Before she left, Veruschka told me not to use the phone because it was bugged.

How shall I describe the hotel décor clearly? Homage to Nuremburg. The hotel was gigantic and the dusky halls were lined with exposed wires; you knew one wrong step in the bleak darkness and you'd be electrocuted. A concierge/jailer sat at the end of my corridor; under the swinging light bulb, this large mound of lard in an apron, with the ankles of a rugby player, tossed me the keys. My room had a toilet – or maybe it was a sink, I couldn't tell – and a flea-infested cot. It was so hot in the room that at night I had to open the fridge and sleep with my feet in the freezer compartment.

The following day, Veruschka said she had to return to London, to minister another dying tourist and I tried to find the face muscles to control my glee. In her place she provided a representative, Anna Vronsky, a beautiful woman, deeply depressed in designer couture. I checked the label of her jacket: Chanel. At 21 Anna was the mistress of Russia's most famous poet, a man in his late fifties. She had borne him a child (the status of poet in Russia is similar to a rock star in the rest of the world). Being unable to send money back to Russia when he toured the capitals of the world, he sent her designer clothes. Her sad little hovel was crammed with couture, but tragically you can't eat a Valentino, or feed it to your kid.

The film we were making was a comedy about me doing horrible stand-up across Russia (Georgia, Sochi, Moscow and the Black Sea). May I remind you here of the ill-fated Nazi invasion of the Soviet Union that ended in the army's collapse when they attempted a tour similar to mine? Since Anna was so beautiful, my director decided to invent a character for her to play in the film. Isn't that always the way? She would play the 'translator', a woman who hated my capitalist guts (as much as I hated her commie ones). In one scene, I had to follow the act of a hundred-member Georgian Dance troop. On stage, they'd been tumbling and doing death-defying cheerleader splits over swords, pointing up. After their standing ovation, my name was announced; I came out, nervously attempting to dodge erect swords, to total silence. I then delivered my lines, 'Hello Georgia, I just want to know if any of you have anything that once belonged to the Wax family? Do you remember them? Short? Jewish-looking people? We left in kind of a rush due to an allergy to death?' I looked over to my translator, Anna, who was shooting me looks from hell, waves of hostility washed over me from the audience, and we exited.

Backstage, we filmed me blaming Anna for her bad translation, as the cause of my performance death, but what really happened after the performances is I'd literally throw up from the awful humiliation of what I'd done. We obviously couldn't tell the audience I was being bad on purpose, that we needed to capture the real looks of disgust. Such is the sacrifice for art. How crazy am I? How crazy was I to become?

I started to love this girl midway through the filming. We were on a grim, black-sanded beach in Sochi, surrounded by gargantuan Russian thighs and flanks when I finally snapped at Anna, 'Why are you always so depressed?'

She replied, 'The pain of living is too much.' Her whole life she had been beaten down by the system until it made her lethargic and she couldn't fight back – her family had been threatened by the KGB to the point that her mother attempted suicide and her uncle died by hanging himself. Her father, a cinematographer, had won an Oscar that the government kept locked away from him in a vault. I couldn't stomach it that she couldn't go in the same restaurants, hotels – couldn't even rent the same beach loungers as the foreign tourists. She just sighed in resignation. Years after filming she told me over the phone, she got MS – 'Finally my insides match my outsides.'

When I got back to London I was overwhelmed by the colours after my black and white Russian experience – I couldn't get over the colours. I remember staring at a red label in duty free, and almost weeping at its beauty. After the Russian diet, I was more ravenous than ever before and roamed London from restaurant to restaurant like a waddling, obese landlocked homing pigeon. I couldn't even wear shoes any more because my feet oozed out the sides as I steamrollered over oncoming pedestrians to get to the next chocolate cake.

When I was nine months pregnant I accepted a job in LA doing a pilot for a TV interview show. Again I said, 'Sure why not, what would be the problem?' Ed had given up arguing with me at this point, and just came along with a bucket. At the LA studio all the costume person could think to do with me was dress me as a gigantic glitter ball. I don't know who I interviewed because I couldn't see them from behind the mountain range of my stomach. I must have been completely demented.

I kept forgetting what I was saying and repeated all the questions more than twice; I would suddenly wake, as if from a dream, and ask whichever celebrity was sitting over the horizon, 'Exactly, what is it you do?' I also did vox pops as filmed inserts. I insisted we visit gangland neighbourhoods to get to know the real LA. Two security men had to carry me through the 'hood' as walking was now beyond my means and it was dangerous for a white person to show their face. When I met members of the gang, I asked if I could come to their clubhouse and did it have a ping-pong table? They didn't kill me; they ran from me thinking I was insane. Needless to say the show was a flop – I was nine months and one week pregnant when I left LA, a doctor had to stick his finger in my cervix to make sure I wasn't about to have contractions aboard the plane. At least, he said he was a doctor.

Before I left for Russia I had bought a house in London from a woman committed to saving wildlife. There were so many disabled creatures stuffed into her basement, it looked like a scene from *Bambi*. Mono-antlered deer, boss-eyed squirrels, blind Labradors, schizophrenic hamsters all roamed freely and urinated freely. When the gardener started to dig behind the house he found wall-to-wall corpses. (Remember the film *Poltergeist*. This was the rodent version.) Needless to say, he quit.

I had found a husband and wife interior decorator team. I wanted to give the house that Santa Fe, New Mexico look, so I showed them pictures of terracotta adobes with farm implements hanging off the wall. Though, in actuality, you need 200 years of bleaching sunlight to create a hacienda, I was determined. And even though the house was Edwardian, they didn't question my judgment.

I had been collecting barnyard tools between trips; in fact I'd never been happier than driving around the English countryside, ransacking farms in the dead of night. I stole pitchforks, scythes, saws, crop shearers, ox neck braces etc. Back at home I spray-painted them black, and hung them up on the walls – friends laughed at me in a worried kind of way.

Once back from LA, I was alarmed to find my house decorated in a Hampstead Jewish version of the Santa Fe look. Instead of following my brilliant, original vision, and giving me a base to hang my contraband rural wall-hangings, the decorators – two Jews from Essex who wouldn't know South of the Border if it came up and bit them – painted big zigzags on tables, lamps, mirror frames and chairs in neon orange, Miami lime green, retina-burning yellow and blinding fuchsia. Everything but the cleaning woman was covered with zigzags.

When you're pregnant there's no such thing as a little irritation, it's always the full frontal lobe, reptilian brain-rage. Once I started screaming at them I couldn't stop, I even attempted to pull the zigzag saw from the wall and kill them.

Nine months, two weeks pregnant and still no sign of anything coming out, who could blame it? Ed was packing his bags and making excuses, like he had important business, in Romania. My food cravings had gone off the chart. At one point I insisted Ed go to Terminal Three at the airport and get me the hot dogs they served there because they tasted American. Ed said, 'But that hot dog place is where you pick up your luggage.' I said, 'Then fly somewhere and get back in there, you fucker.' I had no pity, I wanted it with all the relish and I wanted it now!

Ed and I went to a birthing class – once. The Head Nursie asked, 'How does everyone want to give birth?' I was appalled as each mummy-to-be tried to out-machismo the next one. 'I want to have my baby on all fours, humped over a Ford Fiesta.' 'I want mine hanging from a trapeze with Wagner on the speakers.' 'I want electrodes in the stirrups and a grenade up my ass.'

None of them insisted on pain relief. To me this was insane. Why would you want to be awake for excruciating agony? I don't understand these women who want natural labour. To me it's like going to the dentist and asking for a natural root canal. 'Yeah, just drill straight into my gums, hold the Novocain, I want to be in touch with my teeth.' Are they nuts? If God wanted us to have a natural birth he would have put zippers on our stomachs.

One of the last nights Ed and I were still speaking, he took me to an 'all you can eat' Indian restaurant. I was yelling in my usual *Exorcist* fashion, spewing bile, head spinning and waving a tandoori leg at my husband when my waters broke on a bench I was sharing with a man. A title wave of fluids whooshed out of me. I just shouted 'Surf's up' and the man passed out. Ed dragged me into the street; dogs, squirrels, old women, all washed away in my path. The words 'Oh fuck' did not stop coming from my mouth.

When Ed and I burst into the emergency ward we were both begging for an injection. One nurse tried to bullshit me about the cervix needing to be so many inches dilated before an epidural could be injected in the spine. When I threatened to blow the hospital up, I was hit up immediately. But 17 hours later, I wasn't dilating anywhere. People in green smocks were dropping by to shove their fingers inside me, and walking off shaking their heads. I told them my theory: my body was not made to give birth, but they still wouldn't send me home.

After another four hours of labour, I phoned Alan Rickman while putting on my make-up and told him to get dressed, we were going out for dinner. As we spoke men in green hats gathered around me and interrupted to ask if I would consider a caesarean as the baby was stuck in me. When I asked about the benefits of surgery, they said if I tried to squeeze out the baby, its brains would be so squished we'd be losing a lot of IQ points. I didn't want the low intelligence option so I said, 'Get it out, now,' telling Alan on the other end to order dinner for me, I'd be a little late. I got shot up with a morphine-like substance, which made me as funny as Lenny Bruce; it wasn't exactly stand-up I was doing, it was more lie-down comedy but even so, every doctor gathered at my head to hear the next one-liner. Finally, someone down there at the baby exit, probably the janitor, tugged away and pulled out the baby.

Thank God for caesareans. Not only are the drugs top of the range but I remain almost a virgin and luckily I can still do my 'toss the ping-pong ball' act.

Then I saw Max – there he was this purple, red, yellow mass, arms akimbo, grabbing at the air like he was drowning in oxygen. When they hand the baby to you, you feel this love 'whoosh' through your entire being. It's either pure love, or pure morphine, I can never decide which. Whatever, I felt like the Madonna I was so full of goodness and love.

And now I'm lying with this thing in my arms and he stares at me so solemnly that I want to apologise and promise to start reading up on childcare as soon as we get out of there.

That evening, I woke my hospital roommate with questions, keeping her up all night. 'Why is it leaking? How do you feed it? Can I use your breast for milking purposes?' She seemed to know everything. The next day I was rolled into my own room. I assumed the staff had been talking: 'Oh, she's on television she must want some privacy.' When I told the staff I didn't mind sharing, they responded bluntly, 'No, the woman you were sharing with wanted you removed.'

I remained in my own room for ten days, refusing to leave the hot and cold running, large Jamaican midwives, who knew how to nurture. The following day I got a hospital staff visitor, some woman in a woolly hat, cocooned in a caftan. She lectured me on the beauty of breastfeeding, and stuck the baby on my breast.

Now has anyone got questions about what breastfeeding feels like? I will tell you my opinion. Take a fishhook and pierce it through the end of your mammary, now reel yourself out and dangle by your tips. Another example? Wait for a truck to come by, when it slows down superglue your boobs onto the bumper and shout, 'Giddiup.'

The breastfeeding person told me to feed on demand but I said I'd prefer to have a more Italian opening hours method;

I'd feed a little before lunch, have a long siesta, and then feed maybe once again in the early evening. These were my feeding demands – finito. The bottles were brought out and the nipples were put away.

From this point on, your whole world revolves around smelling the baby's head. You become addicted to this smell. You leave work, turn down sex, even deny yourself food to get another hit; you will kill for this smell. God must put something on that head that stops you from flushing it down the toilet when it screams all night. This bald, pink blob has become the most beautiful thing in the world; you stare at it with constant fascination and love as you inhale deeply.

Once the smell fades what keeps you interested is, I think, your belief that it's a reflection of yourself. Narcissus staring into the water and falling in love is how you gaze into the crib. And when you gradually realise this child is not you – that's where the cracks can start to show and if you're not aware of what's happening, they can end in the full earthquake. Little individual quirks of the baby are like cracks in the San Andreas faultline when the reflection that once adored you back now has the audacity to break ranks and march off to obey the sound of his own bugle call.

This Is A Big Moment.

Now you can either celebrate the phenomenon that you've given birth to an individual and go 'Hurray, it's not me.' Or you can take a mallet and attempt to beat that clay till it looks like you. (It never will.) When Max first said, 'Go away,' during a food argument I could feel my father's and mother's right arm lift into the air, the reptile jaw open and I could hear myself blast him with, 'Do you know what I've done for you? You ungrateful child?' As soon as I recognised what was happening, I shut down the motors, switched off the engines, sent myself to my room and locked the door. Urgently, I jammed on the breaks so that I didn't follow in 'Mommy and Daddy Dearest's' footsteps.

Here's another pitfall you may encounter after childbirth and I've observed this in many close friends: they disappear up baby's ass. It's the 'I don't count anymore but look what I made' philosophy.

So many women I know stopped being interesting once they plotzed out a baby and suddenly only regurgitate this one topic, 'their baby', to the point where I want to scream, 'What about you?' Of course, this would register as incredibly selfish, so I don't scream, I just Tippex them out of my address book. They do, I admit, develop extraordinary party-giving skills. Overnight they become experts in organising the right party bags with colour-coded balloons attached, filled with expensive kazoos, Day-Glo false teeth and edible skeletons. Their feet, however, have been ground to the ankle by the constant running from the kitchen with plates of Pooh-Bear-shaped jellies and peanut butter Goofy-head sandwiches and let's not forget about the booking of the professional clown/pervert who makes rabbits climb out of his pants.

Mostly, the supermom looks exhausted and drained but, goddamn it, she's going to give this kid everything she didn't have and thinks it wants. I always imagine when her kid is older and asks, 'What were you doing when I was young?' She will say, 'Making cupcakes.' What will the kid think? Oh, I want to do that? At least, I'll have a few really good stories to offer up. 'Well, kids, I got in Hugh Hefner's bed. And um … ah … I found Imelda Marcos's second stash of shoes. What about … um … I got O.J. to stab me with a banana.' Will that make them proud? Maybe I'm deluding myself.

Not just the mummy but the daddy too can go up baby's ass. You must have seen these couples. Perfectly normal people suddenly ram photos of a bald, pink head with two eyes into your face and wait for you to respond with, 'Oh, my God, I've never seen anything like that before.' I always want to say, 'It's a head for fuck sake, mine has a head too, what's the big deal?'

I perhaps inherited this attitude from my mother who had a ground zero maternal instinct. Her idea of breastfeeding was putting a bowl of milk in the corner of the kitchen and saying, 'Help yourself.' I remember once we were in a restaurant and a newborn was screaming nearby – my mother zapped her Darth Vader charm at the child. The new mum mistook it for foreplay, for one of those cuddly conversations that go, 'Oooh, what's its name?' 'Her name is Cookie and she's five weeks old, aren't you, Cookie?' 'Isn't she adorable? Can I hold her?' This new mum was holding her child out in anticipation when, suddenly, my mother opened her mouth and from the pits of hell came a voice (said with Austrian accent which makes it more chilling), 'If you don't shut that moron up, I'm going to slam it against a vall!'

My mother didn't even get that maternal thing with my kids. I remember once her saying, 'I think Maxie's just swallowed a rock.' Said as casually as if she was ordering a salad Niçoise; he had been choking for the last five minutes.

From experiences like those above, I knew I might be lacking in nurturing skills. For the first few weeks I carried Max as if he were a clutch bag. I didn't understand the strange ways of babies. After I'd been home with him a month I called the hospital and screamed, 'He's in a coma.' They told me to bring him in; I drove screaming like a siren out the window so everyone ahead got out of my way. Once I had described the symptoms to the doctor – how his head went way back when I picked him up and how he just lay there without movement – I was informed that Max was asleep.

After that I had made it to the weird people list, and received droves of home visitors who came daily to make sure I wasn't killing Max in my ignorance. I once forgot to change him for a whole day, and as I lay him down, excreta started oozing out of his shirtsleeves. I am writing this in shame, and I hope he realises I just lacked the basic skills but thank God I could choose the right nanny. I looked for childbearing thumbs, endless love and those big bosoms that my grand-mother had. I always felt like an amputee who hired artificial limbs. Also I had picked the right husband, who had the skills of the world's greatest mother and father combined. I must have instinctively known when I saw his skinny legs the first time. It was Ed who fed them, dressed them, played with them, read to them, taught them, sang to them, told them stories and gave them love. I had little skill in these areas. I did buy them toys, clothes and made sure they had whatever they needed. This was how I expressed my love. Just in a different way.

In other aspects, I'm not that different to other mothers. I love watching my kids spit mush across the room. 'Look at the curve of spew, isn't he a genius?' I'd shout, but I didn't want to clean it up. To be honest when I tell people I have children and they say, 'You don't seem like a mother', I'm proud: I don't want to be like a mother. You see them outside schools with their fat ankles and their soft white mumsey skin and hair. The fathers (probably younger than me) with the white wispy hair around a yarmulke of baldness, red face like they're going to explode, briefcase, pinstripe suit and with that yaya clippie clip voice that sounds like a peacock barking.

I felt like I was going to get busted if I acted too much like myself, among the mumsey set. Why then did I want my kids to go to school with these people? Every time I meet one of these Westministerian or Oxbridgian daddies and they tell me they got a first in politics, economics and philosophy – the next thing out of their mouths is about the woman in Bangkok who squats on a paper and writes 'Welcome to Thailand' with her vagina. You can bet your bottom dollar, if they were educated at a top school, this is the real object of their fascination. That, and the time their friend Priggers urinated in the headmaster's hat. You wait at least two hours for their guffaws to die down – so much for the hallowed halls of education.

And wifey is just as fascinating – the English mummy who wants Charlie to follow in Daddy's footsteps is so ambitious. Little Charlie is signed up for tennis when he's still wet with afterbirth and at three has a poker up his spine to hold his head erect for piano lessons, and all this makes you think to yourself, *Jesus, if I don't want mine to look like an idiot, I've got to get him on a golf course, right now, and glue some putting irons in his balled up hands.*

When you're in labour, you'll get a message by jungle drums. The drums say, 'It's time to apply to a good primary school or you won't get a place.' I waited till the epidural had kicked in, then made the call. An upper-class voice answered. This voice was so clipped it sounded like a small, mean dog yapping down the phone line at me. When the voice asked, 'Child's birth date?' I panted back, 'Give me a minute, I'm still contracting.' She told me to call back when the kid's genitals showed enough to identify the sex. I was about to hang up when the voice, not so subtly, asked what kind of birth was I enjoying. I knew she was trying to determine how squished the child's brain might be. These days the best schools want only the finest of head, which is pretty ironic, since most of the British Empire is founded on squished heads.

After I emerged from my drug daze, I immediately dialled the school back once I identified the newborn's genitals. The chilling voice at the other end rebuked me for taking so long in labour, saying would I like to go on the waiting list? Snappily, I asked if people had signed up during their scans; she was not amused.

In the end, thanks to Ed's Old Boy connection, Max was accepted as a pupil by his father's primary school and on his first day of school, my heart broke. You take this unique child and dress it in the Nazi Youth 'Mein Kampf' business suit, topped with a natty straw boater that gives the effect that a member of the Gestapo is about to break into a vaudeville routine. And you send him off dazed and confused just like his forefathers were. It was hard for me to swallow. The whole thrust of my life had been to be as unlike my parents as possible.

I didn't even attempt labour with Madeleine, my second child. I booked the day for the caesarean and, with the help of the most fantastic drugs on earth and a knife, out she came. This time I was also smarter on the educational front and got her into the Fort Knox of nursery schools. I went to the interview in full make-up, shaking with fear that I wasn't worthy. Usually they will only accept your child if you are president of Sony, chairman of the BBC or the editor of the *Financial Times*. In truth, I'd applied for Max to go there, but at the time, I was only a comedian on Channel Four with not great viewing figures. We were not accepted. When I went back to beg for Madeleine's possible entry, I had a series on BBC 1 with 7 million viewers, so they said OK you're important enough now to have your child come here to lick blocks.

Every morning, a big rosy woman in an oversized woolly pully asks each precious child, 'What's the "news" today?' The room hushes as Sir and Lady Harvey Nichols video their kid picking his nose, and answering, 'My father won the takeover bid at Glaxon pharmaceuticals, but kept 40 per cent of the equity.' The next one is jumping up and down impatient for her turn and interrupts with: 'My daddy amalgamated his corporate capital turnover at 26.7 of the Japanese fiscal earnings.'

At Fort Knox nursery, I met a new breed of mother. Unlike, the fat-ankled, scone-scoffers at Max's school, this other breed resemble sleek Rolls-Royces. These are the professional wives who don't work, don't do housework and are coated with Prada, Armani, Marni and Solange Azagury jewellery – the good news? The daddies still look like pinstriped old prigs.

All this made me feel like a stranger in a strange land because the rebel in me was never far from the surface. As I said, I grew up in a generation that didn't believe we would ever be adults. The baby boomers that I knew from my hippiedom really didn't go on to make ideal families as seen in the magazines. Every one of my friends from my time at university was and remains 'out there'. Some so rebellious they're still hitch-hiking through Europe, arguing with each other endlessly about what 'I Am The Walrus' means backwards. Others are living in India too stoned to get up; The Magical Mystery Tour came and took them away. We never wanted to grow up and to become an adult was like joining the enemy. To become like your parents was to become a traitor.

So to this day, the word 'parent' fills me with fear. So now I am an adult and worse a parent and when my kids are bad, like when we've just superglued Hula Hoops to our cat Pushka's eyes, we all quake with fear waiting for our mother to come home and give us hell. That's when I suddenly remember with terror, *I am the mother*. That big bird called Maturity has not landed on my shoulders. Where is the training to make you become an adult? Where is the guidebook? I never learned to become Mummy; I didn't study Mummy 202 at Mummy University. You read in those books that tell you by six weeks baby should be able to distinguish between you and your coffee table. Yeah, he can distinguish but what if he likes the coffee table more than me?

I'm always scared my kids will bust me, demanding, 'OK, what the hell do you know about motherhood?' And I'll scream, 'I know nothing, it's a sham. You think I was born knowing how to wipe someone else's ass?' So it was a shock when Max went to school, in suit and tie, clutching his brief-case at the ripe old age of four and there I was, greeted by his principal, so stereotypical, she could have played the head-mistress in those St Trinian's films and when Max wasn't really spelling words in the right order, she gave me, 'We don't like slow boys here. I, of course, came out of the womb spelling "encyclopaedia",' and I wanted to say, 'Well now, look at you, you look like an old man, blowing your whistle once a year at sports day and telling the boys how "jolly well" they all tried. You twat.' She even attempted to direct those horrendous school plays where the students present the parents with samplings of what they've learned at school that term. One particular masterpiece was called, 'The Antarctic.'

CHILD ONE: (*With voice similar to Queen*) Hello, I'm plankton.

CHILD TWO: Plankton is a very important food for the
polar bear.

There was another stunning showstopper about earthworms
and what their habits are.

CHILD ONE: (*Voice of Kenneth Williams*) Hello, I'm a tiny
earthworm.
CHILD TWO: I'm brown.
CHILD THREE: I've got ten stomachs.
CHILD FOUR: I like to burrow in the soil.

The whole extravaganza lasts eight minutes. When I was that age,
we were doing *Oklahoma*. I was in the back row, in full cowgirl
regalia, but upstaging everyone. (No one else was in costume.)

By the time we got to the 'Yip I Yip I, Yip I – A' point in
the song, I had, using elbows and sharpened spurs, squeezed
my way past the chorus and wedged myself between the leads.
When I opened my tasselled arms and raised my beaming face
to the limelight, you could hardly make out anyone behind me.

And my children are doing shows on earthworms? Why? Is
it going to be brought up later at a dinner party?

(To be spoken pucker like you have an earthworm shoved
up your ass.) 'Do you know, Lord Harvey Nichols, that earthworms like to borrow in the soil?'

'Reeeally? How fascinating. Sir British Airways informed me just last week, that they had ten stomachs.'

And about the Antarctic as mentioned before – why are they studying it? We ain't ever going there, it will be melted by the time they're sixteen. Teach them something useful like when a car salesmen is telling you, 'I'm giving it to you for 10,000.' You should say, 'Fuck you, I'll give you 2,000, and you're lucky to get that, you shit.'

No one is giving you anything, they're taking. At least my father taught me how to negotiate and he was a genius at it, he used to try and talk the salesgirl down when buying toothpaste. This is a gift from the Jews but they don't offer that at these prissy schools, only what whales are munching on. This is because the English never think they're going to get screwed like the Jews do, everything seems so lovely and homey, sitting all comfy, in their woolly pully's, having a nice cup of tea with a bickie or a drinkie at elevensies. Some of them not making a penny but they're not panicking because they're going to a 'lovely party', in a 'perfectly lovely frock' and Bedilya is 'soooo funny' and Hugo is 'absolutely maaarvellous.' He's not work-ing, but drives a Jag drinking 'masses of champagne', 'lovely, bubbley, wubbley, champers'. There's such a strength in being English, they're so trusting and hopeful and believe it will all come out in the wash.

Meanwhile, back at the pogrom, the Jews are panicking,

they don't have time for tea and 'drinkies' cause they're always hunting for who's fucking with them, jousting stick erect. Their motto is, 'Fuck them before they fuck you.' When I asked my shrink about this, she said because the English have never been persecuted, they never think someone is coming up behind them to rip them off. In their minds they're all singing the long-playing album, 'There'll always be an England ... never, never, never shall be waved,' accompanied with guns and drums and cannons. In some Dickensian part of their brain, they're thinking, even if things get bad for Oliver, some kind soul at Christmastide will take him to their hearth and give him a nice cup of cocoa, a steaming bowl of spam and chips and miles and miles of sausages.

The Jews know if they knock on a door, chances are big they won't get in; they have knocked on the door of whole countries and were not let in. 'Hello Switzerland, can I come in? I'm about to be fried?'

'Sorry, no room at the inn.'

Obviously, at this point in my life, I still had some issues to address. For the second time in my life, something was not right in the State of Denmark.

9

BREAKDOWN

' Marcel Marceau

THIS SHOULD HAVE BEEN A POINT in life where I took off my hat and threw it skywards, whooping with joy.

But instead of whooping I seemed to be skidding towards an abyss. If it's considered the pinnacle of achievement for a woman to be able to juggle everything, let me annihilate that myth right now. It's not possible – it doesn't work! God or whoever's in charge up there makes out a bill for wanting it all and getting it and you will pay that bill. There will be divine justice for being such a pig (see Greek tragedy).

There were early warnings, but I ignored them.

I was living in the Edwardian house sans zigzag as I had painted them over but the farm implements remained still hanging from the walls. Some things I will never let go of.

After I had lived there three years I made an offer on my dream house. Oh, I forgot I have to say 'we' like married people do. We finally made an offer on my – sorry – 'our' dream house. The house was in a crescent lined with tall, elegant late-nineteenth-century houses; every house was painted in a different muted, pastel colour. The backyards bordered onto a communal, lush, Englishy country-style garden (see film *Notting Hill* where Julia and Hugh sit on our communal park bench).

For years, I had occasionally taken walks around this neigh-bourhood, and I'd stare yearningly into the large, picture windows, thinking if I had a house like one of these, my life would be bliss. Finally, someone obligingly died, and we moved in, just as the ambulance was pulling away.

I was pregnant with my third child, so you can guess at my relaxed state of mind. Just before the move, I came down with bronchitis. I was so sick I could hardly put one foot in front of the other, but even so, because I was so excited to finally be inside one of the large picture window houses, I dragged myself outside into the much coveted communal garden. It was a mere five minutes of bliss as I perused the greenery sitting on Hugh and Julia's bench before my reverie was interrupted by a small child, standing in front of me. The child asked innocently, 'Are you Ruby Wax's mother?' She watched me wide-eyed as I re-crawled my trail back to the house and searched for a knife to open my veins.

Not only I wanted my house, everyone did. We were broken into eighteen times in the first two months. Once I was robbed by someone on crack. They caught him, that's how I know. The good news about people on crack: they think things like Tupperware are really expensive. I was getting jittery.

My breakdown began during sports day. The parents had come in their Range Rovers and laid out their picnic baskets stuffed with champagne and smoked salmon sandwiches, on their tartan blankets to watch Finola skip across a field. I felt like a penguin trying to fit in with a pack of cheetahs, as I wandered lonely from blanket to blanket searching for my lost tribe. It's the same lost feeling I had as a child, back home in Evanston, gazing through the living room window at the park outside, my dog Lumpi at my side, both noses pressed to the glass; that same sense of sadness. That outside lay an oasis of security, happiness and ... barbequing and I would never be able to crack it. Anyway, this is how I'm feeling among these strange English people. I start to watch my child in terror that she feels the same way. Is she blending in? Or does she feel that devastating emptiness too? Does she feel herself to be a freak, like her mother did?

The girlies in their blue shorts have lined up, a gun goes off and the races begin. Everyone jaguar's it towards the finish line, except my daughter, who is pretty much walking while she waves happily to me. She doesn't seem to recognise this is a fight to the death, the thoroughbred mothers have suddenly transformed into Boadiceas, issuing bloodcurdling screams for Finola to run like fuck and my daughter is waving at me, all shiny and smiles; she doesn't give a hoot about heading towards the finish line. At this point I called directory inquiries and asked for the number of the Priory. I should have gone in then, but I didn't. Looking back on it, I now realise she won. The rest are still running for all I know.

Obviously I didn't go nuts because my kid didn't win a ribbon at sports day; no, that would make me too crazy. It was more that a day of reckoning had arrived; I had wandered far, far away from my original blueprint, of kid in the playground, but in rewriting and expanding her role I'd gone too far into the dark woods and couldn't find my way back. Let me pile on another metaphor – I can't dance, but if I'm near someone good I can copy them like a dream. I can even create the illusion that I'm having a good time, but when they leave the floor I quickly have to find someone else to mimic.

I was walking around on sports day, passing blanket after blanket, thinking how I had lived my whole life this far as a reflection of other people. I became what each and everyone expected from me, I always thought I was such a rebel, but no, I had unwittingly sold my soul for approval. I wanted to click my heels together and say, 'There's no place like home' and be there, but where exactly was home? I had run away from home and besides that's where the wicked witch of the West lived, so why would I be clicking for that?

When you start to think like this, here's a tip: check into your nearest clinic. But there was no one to give me this advice, I wanted so much to turn to those people scoffing salmon sandwiches and ask, 'Is it just me or do you feel insane? How are you acting your part so well? How do you live your life, and can I have some?'

When you have a mental disorder, in other words are sick in the head, the big double whammy is you can't tell you're ill, because when the very brain that makes these assessments is infected, it can't give a correct reading. No one's second-in-command – no one. If you had a spare brain it would tell you you've gone nuts, but you don't; here's the bitch: you are what's wrong with you.

I had a vague feeling I wasn't right in the head as everything was difficult. You can't make decisions about anything: what to eat, what to wear, whether to turn left or right at a street crossing. Everything is hard because you're living as someone else.

Before sports day, another clue that my mind had abandoned the mother-ship was my decision to redecorate my new house. I suppose my belief was that if I could just get the outer landscape right, the inner would not be far behind.

I had become obsessed with colour schemes. Many of you might know this but I didn't; when you choose a paint, there is no such thing as beige. At the expensive paint shop you're presented with infinite strips of off-white samples that all look exactly the same to the naked eye. Confused, I covered my house and my husband in colour swatches: Dusky Tijuana Marshmallow, Burnt Desert Sunrise, Peachy Devon Crème, Baby Bottom Squishy Taupe – but they all look beige. Maybe a bat with its radar vision could detect a difference, not me. But I wanted the perfect colour, I'd keep showing up at the paint shop and they'd go, 'Hide, it's her again. Pretend we're statues.'

This is a sure sign of a nervous breakdown, when the mind can only focus on hairline borders of beige. If this happens to you, call a doctor immediately; I know I am not alone in this. When I finally entered the Priory, there were others, striped with paint swatches across their bewildered faces, asking questions like, 'What's the difference between Tawny Bronzed Beige and a Magnolia Dewdrop Off White?'

This is not the way I would have liked to go crazy. I had

always hoped that if I went nuts, it would be in that deep Kafkaesque existentialist angst, volcanic way, caused by the fact you've realised life has no meaning, so you 'Sylvia Plath' it over to the aga and try to steam-fry your head. But no, my angst derailment was due to the fact that I was redecorating my home and wanted to find a suitable beige for the bathroom. I tried to squeeze out these horrible mundanities like a pimple but they would not budge. I'd wake up in a sweat, clutching samples, wondering whether I should go with a Sunny Buffy Mexican or just a plain old Clam Chowder, or maybe just dive off the deep end and go into the Prune family? I did jump off the deep end but didn't end up with Prune, I ended up with Priory.

The minutiae of life started eating me alive; I had lost the big picture. I knew this because my life became consumed by making lists and when one thing got crossed off the list, more things grew in its place. I was holding on to sanity by giving myself 'things to do': buy toilet paper, change light bulb, get car washed, clip children's toenails, brush teeth. The inside of my head became like Hong Kong: strobing neon on big billboards flashing day and night, day and night. Each thing seemed as important as the next; shave legs, write comedy show, have baby, write thank you notes, book dinner, go to India to find self, another baby coming through, have sex with husband, buy toilet paper, maybe change husband, grow fingernails, paint hair beige …

I'd meet people at dinner parties and they were, say, yabbering on about earthquakes in Uzbekistan – I'd scrunch up my face and try to look all concerned and serious, but really I couldn't stop thinking, 'Where can I buy those donut-shaped corn plasters?'

Also I was pregnant for the third time. Did I mention that? It wasn't helping my clarity any. I tried, like the self-help books said, to picture gold light shining in my stomach, so that whoever was down there wouldn't feel the turmoil above. She was floating in the darkness and so was I. We were both as unborn as each other; two survivors floating in the icy waters around the *Titanic* trying to help each other out and, sure enough, it manifested physically because whatever is in the mind is in the body. The doctor said something's not right – 'Her growth is diminishing, and the embryonic fluid around her is drying up.' I thought my mind was sapping her strength, like a succubus drinking her energy. As the baby kicked and wanted out, I wanted out too. I told the doctor I saw only black at this point, that I had lost my way. Needless to say, once Marina was born, rather than the usual medical team circling me, I had a circle of shrinks.

They all agreed with me, that something upstairs wasn't right. The baby was fine, the mother was not. They made me see a psychiatrist as soon as I could stand upright. A tsunami of despair had washed over me, and whoever made the mental

Lumpi and me at the picture window, sharing a happy moment.

First shag (see page 65).

The first Alan in my life
(see page 52).

The very lovely Alan Rickman, Carmen DuSautoy and Ian Charleson, sunning themselves when there was still an ozone layer.

The nubile Alan Rickman and me admiring our names outside the Royal Shakespeare Company (see page 93).

On plastic in Miami (see page 35).

Me as barmitzvah woman in *The Tempest* for the
Royal Shakespeare Company (see page 94).

Early wench-work in *Love's Labour's Lost* at the
Royal Shakespeare Company (see page 93).

In *The Maids* in Glasgow.

Girls on Top – with some other people, I can't remember their names.

Our wedding day ... and later (overleaf), when Ed found out what the deal really was.

decisions was uncontactable; the pilot of the *Enterprise* had deserted his post.

I was finally thrown out of the hospital two weeks after giving birth to Marina because the administration said someone else needed the room, but I wanted to stay forever. I was starting to grow my toenails into the springs, to anchor myself to the safety of the mattress.

A few weeks later, after trying hard to act normal, I asked the nanny at home, 'Do you think there's something wrong with me? Be honest,' and she replied, 'Well, you're glazed and babbling, so maybe.' Now you might think as I did, 'You don't just call a clinic and just say you're glazed and babbling.' But it turns out, you do.

When they told me to come on in, I thought I'd just drive myself there for a quick visit; but somehow I ended up at a betting office in Richmond. Then I thought why not? I could just live in Richmond and work in a betting office. Luckily, someone in the betting shop drove me the rest of the way to the Priory.

I entered the Priory, not knowing what to expect. All the way up the long leafy drive I was expecting to see inmates running across the lawn, and being tackled to the ground by beefy security men types in mucus-green gowns, but it looks like an off-white fairy castle with turrets; the illusion is only broken by the bizarre modern wings. Inside the glass doors, there is a huge chandelier on the foyer ceiling and on arrival, you could think, for a moment, you've come to a spa.

You're lead down the hushed hallway by Nursey with a cupcake hat, who talks to you in the soft, runny voice of a fantasy mummy. She sounds like she really loves you and will take care of you till you die. You enter your womb/room, all shag pile with a little bed and a picture of a mountain on the wall, and you think yes, I'm finally home. Then many cup-caked Nursies come and go, asking questions about your symp-toms and you grapple with answers, rambling in a stream of consciousness way about: (the following is said at top speed without stopping for breath) not knowing if you're sick or not, maybe this is your imagination, you left your purse at home and you have to make about 29 phone calls 'cos you've organ-ised a dinner party that night, so maybe this is a mistake you being here and you're so sorry you're taking up room 'cos clearly someone crazier than you should be occupying this room and you're worried you might not have packed the right things and oh no, you've packed a pyjama bottom and nothing else and can you go to the gym? – because you have to work out –and would they let you film this place 'cos this would make a great documentary and do they have a tennis coach 'cos you should take up a sport and then you'd be fine.

There's an enormous silence, before you're asked how you feel and you tell them as accurately as possible: 'You know how when a turtle opens its eyes, but there's still a layer of skin covering the eye? Well, that's how I feel. Like I'm not really here. Like I'm imagining the world.' Then the doctor shoots you up with a syringe and you hear him say, 'This is not your imagination, you are sick, but not to worry,' and then … and then … out.

You wake a few days later, feeling you don't ever want to leave this room, you're free to go to the cafeteria but by now you don't want to see anyone because you know people are your poison. You're afraid to stoke your addiction for approval; you've just gone cold turkey. One hit – you'd start showing off to someone and get that hit of approval – could send you back to square one.

This new sensation of being alone is a pleasurable one. Suddenly your eyes can focus on print, you can actually read the words and you find they make sense – this hasn't happened for years. You start to form opinions that must be your own because there is no one else around. 'I like this book, I don't like that one.' The pilot is back at the control panel, thank God. This is beyond pleasure, you are with you, and you are such great company.

Gradually, a curiosity long buried perks up its head and you wonder, who else is here? So reluctantly you foray like a frightened dog into the cafeteria with the feelings you had when you were eight, that no one will want to sit with you. But you, like a brave little soldier, go in just like your first day at nursery school, and one kind soul says can they sit next to you? and you're shy and grateful, but can't find the old shtick you used to spin the magic with. The person looks the way you feel and you tell them that you don't know what to eat, or say, or look like and they say, 'Me too.' And there it is: finally you are with your tribe.

Your people. You look in their eyes and find the same look that's in your own, the look that says they've been carrying the big question, 'How do you live this life?' and they don't know. And you realise you had to go to a nuthouse just to finally talk about this question and the fact that you have no idea. You've been yearning to discuss it and you realise everyone on the outside has done everything, memorise every fucking informational highway fact in the universe and statistic on global economy and how many nuclear weapons we actually have, just to avoid this question.

But here in the land of crazies that's all they are talking about – it's the gossip, it's the news. By day three you're laughing; you're so happy, happier than you've ever been in the outside world; here we all have the same point of view. You laugh in recognition when the inmates tell you how they ground to a halt at the supermarket, in the car, at their birthday party, caught in the angst of what the fuck they are doing in this life. Even the seemingly boring housewife was fuelled with existentialist angst and angst to me has always been a sign of intelligence. There were a few like myself who based their entire self-esteem on their job and had a collision. I even met a fellow inmate who also had her breakdown during sports day. Her kid came in second to last.

And upstairs are the addicts, who share such horror stories at night, as we smoke around the campfire, that they provide constant mouth-dropping entertainment. Of course it makes you feel relieved. 'At least I'm not a junkie.' From the other wing come the anorexics, or 'twinkies' as they're called – always with a fabulous supply of food they've been storing for the winter. My favourite junkie had been a concert pianist, a historian and a doctor, a woman so glamorous she'd make *Ab Fab*'s Patsy look shabby. I watched her going cold turkey in a Chanel suit, chain smoking and telling stories of waking up in doss-houses and writing her own prescriptions for heroin. Of getting caught in barbed wire and electrocuting herself while chasing hedgehogs. Of fucking Rich Arabs for money and waking up with people she'd never met.

Meanwhile, various inmates tried to escape, so there's a constant stream of male nurses carrying in the runaways, who were always smiling evilly, as if they wanted to be caught all along. All had parents who behaved at home like Attila the Hun, and yet it was the children who carried the guilt, who feared being 'no good' inside.

There was a patient hierarchy at the Priory: lowest down were the depressives who were considered wankers by the top dogs – the addicts. They thought our illness was more mental (like theirs wasn't?). They had a real chemical to battle with while we only had our thoughts to make us sick. The twinkies were somewhere in the middle. It was like war of the weirdos.

The classes I thought, if I'm going to review the place, weren't the 'specialty of the house', but some of my happiest moments were over the abundant bouquets during Flower Arranging, where we all discussed how crazy we were from living our lives and it's like helium balloons lift off your soul, because this is what you always wanted to be talking about. Even the Therapy Sessions were packed with irony. I remember some Nursey drawing pictures on a flipboard of a sad person and saying, 'This is you,' to all of us. She then asked us what some signs of depression were. One guy who ran some huge corporation, answered, 'Blinking during TV ads.' Then another depressive added, 'Having an urge to lick cats.' I loved my people. I was in a club I liked at last and I didn't have to be funny. They liked you more when you conversed from the bottom of the basement and the deeper you went the more it was admired. And because of this freedom, the light returned to all of their eyes and when I looked in the mirror I could see it returning to mine.

I thought, 'I never want to be sick again' and I thought that it was time to examine my life, to see exactly when and why I let go of the reins.

10

FIXING YOURSELF

Ok, do you want the funny stuff or should I tell you what really happened in my life? I had one foot in doing shtick and one trying to find reality. I'll give you the funny stuff first and then we'll plummet together.

All through my childhood I'd been sent to various counsellors, social workers, specialists in crazy children, who would try to fix me. When I was about nine years old, my teacher thought my school pranks had reached a psychotic level. For a science project I built a volcano (out of papier mâché and baking soda) that really erupted and spewed its contents on innocent victims. During biology I hoarded the organs of many frogs, lovingly placing them on lunch trays, handbags and into the boys' pants. I remember the school counsellor delicately suggesting I draw stick figures to show what 'was going on at home'. I would draw scenes of Saturday afternoons at the Waxs, where my father would beat up mommy and mommy would beat up me, while grandma was trying to bite my mother to get her off me. I loved the sympathy I received so much that I started exaggerating the drawings. Daddy hacking mommy to pieces, grandma being humped by the dog, the dog eating mommy. It backfired. The guy cancelled my appointments, saying he wasn't qualified enough to deal with this case.

My parents sent me to Sunday school where the children studied the suffering of the Jews. Suffer, suffer, suffer. The whole religion seemed based on a whine. OK, so they were always pestered and persecuted but why didn't they just take it on the chin like in England? Or bravely go down with the ship? The Jews made whole holidays around how much they suffered – at Passover we had to eat horseradish to remind us of our bitterness, like we need to be reminded? Bitterness is in our DNA. Also we'd eat matza to help us remember having our asses chased out of Egypt (the reason it's flat is we had to flee so quickly, our bread didn't have time to rise). Of course the sea parted for us and crashed in on the pursuing armies, that's what you get for not letting us finish baking our bread. Ha ha.

I didn't really concentrate at religious school, the whining got to me. I hated synagogue and used to howl like a dog whenever the Cantor sang some hideous Hebronic drone. He always accompanied his dirge by blowing a shofar (it sounds like a cow being tortured). I used to have hours of pleasure after the service asking, 'Who blew the chauffeur?' Needless to say, I was kicked out for bad attitude to stand in the corridor. It was boring and to amuse myself I started playing with switches in a nearby fuse box. The next thing I was aware of was the Rabbi grabbing my elbow and dragging me back to the synagogue. He pointed above the altar. The 'eternal light' was no longer eternal – it was Off. I was sent to see a Jewish educational counsellor for crazy Jewish children who informed me, 'Like a clockmaker makes a clock, so God made us.' I didn't get it … he thought I was amoral and suggested my parents take me to another religion.

OK, that was the funny side of therapy; then it came after me and bit me in the ass. I left the Priory thinking, *No, sweetheart something is really wrong with you – you need healing just like all these lost souls do.* I think W.C. Fields didn't really say this, but it was sort of like it: 'There's a seeker born every minute' and I was just the same as the other shoppers for salvation. We were all looking for some relief from life. Perhaps I was a bit more discriminating about who would heal me. I clearly wasn't handing my psyche over to some quack of a Third Kind, someone who didn't just tie a dead crow on my head, or suggest I dance naked and hump the air to tapes of menopausal whales. I found someone who holds a doctorate in clinical psychology. Call me crazy but I thought it better to play safe.

I found Dr Rosalie Mishkin who lived in the heart of Chelsea and held therapy sessions in her living room. My first impression was that this sixtyish Jewish New Yorker in a tailored pant suit, conventional pearls around her neck, couldn't possibly navigate the mind. She looked like a friendly aunt who makes you cookies. I thought I'd outsmart her in one session, she was too sweet, too normal. I'd just give her the condensed version of my life story and she'd say 'poor you', 'what a wonderful person you've turned out to be, off you go'. She didn't; she just listened blankly. So I worked harder to get her to like me and for the first few weeks each session was a one-woman show, about me, my parents, my job, Ed, my kids (basically all the stuff you've been reading about in this book), complete with one-liners. I think I even paused for the laughs, but they never came. Rosalie never even looked impressed, just looked at me in a sort of pitying way. After a few weeks she spoke:

'How do you feel about all this?' Suddenly I had no lines, no feelings, nothing. She had done the unthinkable. She had taken the magnifying glass I used to study everyone else's foibles and turned it onto me, and when I looked it wasn't a pretty sight – I was just all brain and mouth, I had no feelings. Over time, we pushed the 'down' button, and plunged direct to the heart of darkness.

It was the right time to go 'down'.

I realised by then I'd been living my life like some gun went off at a starting line and I'd been driving at turbo speeds with no brakes and a few breakdowns, only to avoid looking directly at what I was doing. Actually, while I'm on this topic, I know very few people who know how to live their lives – I mean it's not like we get instruction manuals on our exit from the womb.

We don't even have the benefit of one of those old Frisbee-lipped witchdoctors of the tribe who tells us: 'Here is the way to wisdom my child. Now go into the forest and hang from a tree by your earlobes and it will come.' Maybe this is a good thing since our lobes would be dragging around by our knees, which means we'd be wise but we'd look like hell.

And on top of it, I come from a generation that never thought we would grow up, let alone get wise. So in order to avoid it we all dress like kids, we hit the gym and thanks to certain moisturisers and professional men's savvy with a surgical hacksaw, we can look young almost till death. No matter what has to stapled, sewn up or sucked out, the silent message that ain't so silent is: 'Be young, free and don't tell anyone how old you are.' Wisdom is never mentioned in *Vogue* and no one's requesting it at Harvey Nichols.

I'd noticed in my friends that after the age of about 45, the road divides and you can either drive toward madness or toward wisdom. If I wanted to swerve towards wisdom, I'd have to turn that wheel away from where I was headed, quickly.

It was getting late in the day. I had to enlighten up, fast. I knew that I couldn't change my past, but before I could slam the accelerator down again and zoom on towards the rest of my life, I had to see where I'd come from and who I was. Rosalie held up the mirror and gradually over time I saw that I'd created a two-dimensional character, a fabrication. Like those smiling placards of showgirls they put up in Vegas, it was just a show front and behind the front no one was at home. Each friendship has been a gig, where I had to win the seal of approval, winner of 'greatest person I've ever met' award. I had never considered her question, how do I feel about anything, my only thought was did this person like me? Friendships were indiscriminate, I'd flirt with anyone, mentally go to bed with them. Needing them to like me, just to fatten the address book and the amounts of beeps on my answer machine determined how loved I felt that day.

For years, when I'd get home from running myself ragged from engagements, those blinking red lights would warm my very fibres, like sitting around a hearth and roasting marshmallows. But in the end, here I was with this woman, realising my petrol tank was empty, drained from the exertion of keeping the balloons of self-deception afloat. I had spent the energy recklessly, in the desire to please.

I went to a shrink once before, who told me she used to be a film editor until she changed her career at 48. When I asked if there was a connection, she said yes, she helped people make their final edit. Just like with film, she could take hours of mayhem and discard unnecessary action, to reveal the main plot line, just keeping the story clean and simple.

So it was with Rosalie. She could separate my garbage from the gold and hear exactly what was wrong with the engine.

I'd felt for a long time I was floating in a bubble, detached with no feelings whatsoever, as if I were acting out my life rather than living it. She'd make me communicate with this bubble, asking it who was in there and I'd beg her, let me be funny, let me get back in my groove, but no, she made me stay there. I begged her to please not take my cynicism away; it was how I made my living, my reason for living. It would be like taking a pencil away from an architect – who would I be without my ammo? She pointed out, if I didn't fix myself now, I would be paying another call to the Priory. So I sat up and listened.

I realised that I had had a feeling of numbness for years, mini versions of what happened before the Priory. I just hadn't known what it was. Since I was twenty, I would occasionally become ill and I'd have to take to my bed for up to six weeks. I always thought it was glandular fever, or as happened in LA, Epstein Barre.

I would stop feeling like my usual self and begin to feel like something else entirely. It would start with a feverish feeling, then my eyes would go into a stoned-like glaze and my mind felt like it was moving through treacle. Unlike the flu, it didn't pass; it would last for weeks, sometimes I'd get the illness when I was writing, then everything would slow down and my fingers on the computer would pour out lines of childlike banality. I'd be sapped of all my juices: creativity, wit, and intelligence … all gone.

It happened once when I was interviewing during a film about the English upper classes called *The Season*, when I really needed my full artillery of wit to joust with those yipping yayas. But immediately I went into that hazy bubble-state and when I reached for the humour throttle, nothing happened. I was touring Glyndebourne, Henley, Ascot, aware of the bemused faces of those I was interviewing as they wondered why I was asking such stupid questions. Their distain sent me further and further into the abyss, I was mortified that what I felt would be visible on the camera. I remember asking a polo player while the cameras were running, 'Just because you whack a ball with a mallet does that mean you're not going to die?' Jesus Christ, I thought, who was writing my lines?

When I was relating this to Rosalie, I suddenly remembered these feelings from even further back, that I'd actually felt in childhood. Whenever I felt victimised or extremely frightened, I'd go into this slow, treacly state. And I remember, as a child, I'd secretly given it a name. I'd say to myself, 'Oh, yes I'm going into the Mitzi state.' The name Mitzi reminded me of those sad, badly ripped rag dolls that flop over when you pick them up.

Then Rosalie said, try and feel what she feels. Was this shrink out of her mind? I wanted to stab Mitzi in the neck, peel her skin off and tear her eyes out, I wanted to rip her from my insides and throw her as far away as possible, but the threat of the Priory loomed large. As Rosalie said, 'Madness is not an option.'

A disclaimer: I am not a schizophrenic. I am many things but not that; I wasn't two separate people. Mitzi is just a ghost-like feeling, almost like you're visualising a memory. Gradually I could hear a faint 'Edgar Allan Poe-ish' knocking at my chamber door and I knew that it was the kid from the playground. I couldn't believe it. The original me – the tusk-toothed child, her face smashed to the window, demented with loneliness and self-hatred – was still there. You assume that you shed your past like old skin, you don't. She was like some crippled little sister I'd bolted in a coffin many years ago. The fear was almost paralysing as I thought, *Jesus Christ, what if she makes a comeback?* I hated her then and now she could ruin me professionally. It was like having a horrible dummy of yourself, filled with all your deepest fears, what if she just starts mouthing off? Talk about a *Twilight Zone* episode.

And so we analysed why I'd left Mitzi behind. I'd grown up in a madhouse, probably frightened to death; so this child, Mitzi, hid behind someone that could deal with the madness: Ruby. My father reminding me constantly, 'Look at you! You're just a simple-plain-stupid-slow-dumb-pathetic-idiotic-useless-irresponsible misfit. You'll be institutionalised by the time you're 50.' He used to say to my friends, 'Ask Ruby about any news item, she knows nothing' and suddenly I couldn't comprehend the newspaper. He got what he wished for. I lost the ability to take in information – I didn't know anything. I failed at school in politics, literature, languages, maths and history.

My heart got hard and mean and Mitzi went deeper inside and Ruby stepped out to fuck over that woman-hater, he might be destroying my mother, but he was not going to get me. Not that Mommy was any solace to me. Thinking about it I had two killer sharks as parents. When I'd go to my mother for comfort she'd curse me: 'I'm living with a moron; she's just like her father' and I became like him, I invented a 'Dictator Daddy' inside me. Ruby reared her head and said, 'I'll show you. I'm not just going to get a husband, I'm going to get a series.' While Mitzi hid, Ruby kicked their asses for crushing the spirit of idealism and hope inside her. Other kids were doing 'childhood', while I was building a monster.

Ruby was a fabrication – she didn't even need oxygen, she just needed attention from as many people as she could grab. This makes for an exhausting life, but a fantastic career. I had always wondered why I felt so comfortable in front of 3,000 people but not so comfortable in my kitchen loading the dishwasher (see fame and the illness factor). I realised I'd spent the first half of my life creating a front and I'd have to spend the second half tearing it down.

So I asked Rosalie, 'Now that I know Mitzi, can I get rid of her? Can you make her go away?'

'No,' she said, 'I can't.' For me to get better, she said, Ruby and Mitzi would have to unite, cohabit.

I asked, 'Well, what can this Mitzi bring to the table?'

Rosalie said, 'Heart'. Now, heart is something I had never worked with. You certainly don't need heart in television. As a matter of fact, the less heart, the more successful you become as you can stamp on people with the greatest of ease, with no remorse.

The other option was to remain as I was. This is the bitch about therapy – once you've unearthed the unconscious thought you can never bury it again. It shines like a beacon in your head; it demands to be addressed. I could clearly see how

'Ruby', having little heart or feelings, had built a career upon criticising other people, I honestly could never figure out why people told me I was abrasive. I'd say, 'What are you talking about? I was being funny', but when I watched my interviews on tape, I could see myself doling out tiny homeopathic doses of rage to my subjects.

Much of my conversation was sprinkled with cruelty; I could see how my playfulness was sugar-coated abuse. I was worse with the men I interviewed, especially the men who reminded me of my father. If they were successful, rich and charismatic I'd re-enact my relationship with my father, always trying to outsmart them, outwit them, but in the end bending backwards to ensure that they'd like and forgive me. I'd dance and twirl and subliminally kick their bollocks off and in the end win their approval. Some of these interviews seemed more like bullfighting than conversations. I remember after my father's beatings, I'd hug him for comfort and this made the connections of love, pain and fear, twist. When someone expressed love to me I'd feel fear, when someone punished I'd feel loved. The circuits needed rewiring.

When things were going well in my life, I felt invincible; one sniff of failure and I would spiral into a deep depression. That critical voice I had turned on others would suddenly turn on me, berating me for being an 'idiot', 'a loser' and a 'sad sack' – I used to joke on stage: 'I'm in litigation with my inner child', the artillery of spears and arrows, so effective at lancing others, suddenly turned on me. The harsh voice of the father criticising the child can never be erased. I carried his voice all my life, 'Daddy is always right', no matter how much you learn later to the contrary, so I took the whip from his hand and kept lashing.

Then I got addicted to my rage; it was exhilarating at first, like a drug. It's fantastic; you're like the monster in *Alien*, razor-teethed jaws parting, as you salivate for blood. It was delicious until it poisoned me. Later, when you're left with the pain of remorse it's excruciating and the backwash of adrenalin swirls around with no place left to go but back down your throat – this makes for a gruesome hangover.

And this isn't just me, many people I know love to spew anger. *Note*: if shrink tells you to release your anger and you'll feel better, walk away right now, close the door and do not look back. The more rage you let out, the more you make. There is an endless supply of fury in us and if you push the 'anger' button it will continue to flow. It's like saying if you have sex constantly you'll lose your taste for it.

Rosalie convinced me that the road to sanity was to control the beast, to rein in the wild horses that drag the chariot. The beast in us all tries to convince us to unleash the full fury of our frustration because it tastes so good, but our job is to make sure it's the civilised adult in the chariot, to pull in the reins until the rage is suppressed.

I had no prototype to follow. To learn to be this parent when your own parents have acted like children is almost impossible. But someone inside you has to calm you down when you get into that frightened rage, someone must quell its panic when this child-like thing snatches for immediate gratification. I had to replace that critical dictator's voice with a calm, patient one in order to deal with life's inevitable frustrations.

Again, this isn't just me. Many people are fuelled with the 'I want, I want' mantra. We're encouraged by everything around us to 'have it all', eat it all, drive it all, wear it all, have sex with it all, this is what makes us crazy – to live in a state of wanting. As I said, the reason the famous get ill is because they are constantly fed, every material want is satisfied and so it just swells their need for more … and we envy them? The only way towards inner peace is if we learn to be OK when we don't get something, to be OK in the frustration of not getting something or being someone else.

Also, and this was Rosalie's genius, she taught me how to communicate my needs without having to become the little dictator. It's important to describe feelings but to release rage only creates more rage. I wouldn't say I'm an expert at this but at least I have the manual for a change.

With the adult at the wheel, calmness reigns. When fear subsides, rage subsides and you're left with the knowledge that you're safe. You are home and finally it's a safe place – this is the ideal of therapy.

During my time with Rosalie I became the mother of three kids. The main reason I stayed in therapy so long was the fear of passing my rage onto my kids; I came from a long line of 'I'm doing this for your own good' terrorists. My own father had been abused during his childhood, he tried to train me as if I were a wild dog, with beatings and threats and we all know this could be the groundwork for training a pitbull to become a killer. If the discipline is too severe, the child will become either infuriated, deceitful, fearful or it's spirit will be crushed.

Sometimes I could feel my parents' rage burning in me when my kids frustrated me. I could almost taste my mother's words, 'I want respect, I'm your mother. Without me you wouldn't be here, you ungrateful animal.' Ed would take over while this storm raged in me. Afterwards I'd try to explain, 'Mommy's got something wrong with her ... promises to be cured soon ... sorry ... crazy in the head ... get back to me in a few years, you'll like me then.' As gruelling as it was to control myself, the result is: my kids don't express inappropriate anger or have an insatiable desire to please others. Of course, this means they probably won't be going into show business. Such is the mark of a great shrink.

I was with Rosalie for about seven years. During that time my parents would come to visit five or six times a year. In addition I had to visit them on holidays because of their constant badgering, 'We're not going to live long.' May I mention here that that was 250 years ago and they are both still alive? The harbingers of doom would announce themselves via my answer machine: 'Your father and I are coming British Airways, 2:00, Ruby are you listening? British Airways 2:00. 2:00 British Airways. Ruby? Ruby? 2:00 not 3:00 ...' A few minutes later another call came in with more panic in the voice, 'Hello Ruby? Make us reservations at the Hilton. We want to stay on the sixth floor, two beds, not facing the street. Ruby? Not on the street, the sixth floor, two beds, Ruby?' My father would follow up with another call, 'Ruby, this is Chicago calling.' Click. He sounded so angry I thought I was up for multiple murder.

So there I'd be at the airport, late as usual for their arrival, but there. My mother would come out of customs, more hunchbacked and haggard-looking each year, pushing her equally ageing Louis Vuitton suitcases on the trolley. My father strolled out, pushing nothing, looking debonair and snappy in those Fifties American businessman hats, elegant Harris Tweed jacket, tie and overcoat and when my mother would see me she'd look up and screech, 'Vooooooooobbbbbbbyyyyyyyy! I'm here!' Like I could miss her, like anyone in the airport could miss her and for that moment I was filled with love for both my parents. In the car I'd still be thrilled to see them like a little girl pleased with her report card. I'd try to tell them of my recent successes but I don't remember much of a reaction from either parent. Then as we were pulling out of the garage, my father would launch into, 'So, how much money have you got?' I would become ten years old:

Me: 'A lot daddy, I have a lot of money.'
Him: 'How much?'
Me: 'Um ...'
Him: 'You don't know how much? You see Ruby, anybody could take advantage of you because your head isn't screwed on.'

Then we'd be on the motorway, '... I'm your father I won't always be here to protect you. But I've got to tell you, Ruby, some day you're going to be a bum with nothing because you're not responsible.' Then we pulled off the motorway at Chiswick and he's still going, '... I'm leaving you some money but you won't know what to do with it. Running with these insubstantial friends as you call them ... they are bums!' As we enter Notting Hill Gate, '... Ruby, when you're not cute anymore and you're 50 or 60 you'll be crazy like your mother and you'll need the money.'

Pulling up in the driveway: 'Someday they'll see you're a kook and they'll fire you from your television show.'

As Ed opened the car door in time to hear the last few insults, he'd pitch in with, '... Mr Wax that's exactly the reason they hire her.'

My father would answer, entering the house with, 'Well, it's England, who else have they got here? If they could get Frank Sinatra, she would be off the air.' You can't argue with that.

My mother would then ask, looking around, have I cleaned my house and was I still fat? Trying to change the subject I'd tell her the kids were still at school and she'd break into a strange repetitive monologue: 'Maxie's my favourite, he fascinates me, he's like Lumpi was. I find him fascinating, absolutely fascinating.' (To be said with mile long cigarette dangling from lips.)

Five minutes later, I'd push them out of the house, back into the car and drive furiously to the Hilton to check them in and if, God forbid, the room faced the street or it wasn't on the sixth floor, they would have to be moved.

That night I'd have to pick them up again and take them home to see the grandchildren. My father would give me the usual dissertation about how he never thought I'd get anyone to marry me, let alone consent to have kids with me. 'I can't believe it, you were such a sad sack.' He would go on about how happy I had made him and how proud he was that I had reproduced. At times like this, I wanted to throw my arms around him and say, 'I love you, Daddy,' but I restrained myself, knowing that it was always when I was at my most vulnerable that my father would attack.

Sure enough, back at the house, my father would be sitting at the kitchen table with Max who would start crying and suddenly my father would ask what's wrong with Max? 'There's something wrong, he's too sensitive, he's getting hysterical over nothing. Also he can't read.' Max was two at the time.

Julia, the sassy New Zealand nanny, would protest, 'But Mr Wax, you just poked him hard, of course he's crying.' My father would flat out deny it. 'I didn't touch him.' My father wanted Max to lose control, so he would be able to blame me for passing my neurotic genes to his grandson then he'd have a reason to start disciplining him at once. He'd warn me, if I let Max continue his over-sensitivity, he would become as highly strung as I was, hoping and fearing this would happen all at the same time. I would retort, as if I were still ten, 'Maxie's very smart, he's going to go to Harrow some day.' My father would roll his eyes. When he went to grab Max to sit him on his lap, Max would struggle away, still crying. My father would then blame me for putting these ideas in Max's head. (*Note*: Max presently attends Harrow.)

By the time Ed came home from work, the house would be brimming with repressed fury dating back forty years. He would try to humour everyone, to create the illusion of normality, thanking my mother for cleaning the floor as she was still down there with the sponge wiping the corners. Ed would then suggest dinner, inadvertently triggering the next battle – my mother would jump up gleefully, shouting, 'I vant to go to the Italian. I like their bolognaise and Tony who runs it is so charming.' So off we'd go to this horrible crap basement bistro where Tony the charmer puts his tongue in your ear while giving the specials of the day, my mother, throughout the whole dinner, giggling like a schoolgirl.

These outings always ended with a monologue about world politics. My father's delivery reminded me of Imelda Marcos's. To prove a point she used to stick her knife in the dining table. So, with my father who'd stab the table with a fork, shredding the linen to demonstrate the destructive nature of communism. At the end of his tirade he would be dripping with sweat, satiated.

Sometimes Alan Rickman and Rima his long-time girlfriend joined us for dinner. Rima is a very left-wing economics professor. On these special occasions, my father would get out a carving knife and gouge out the wood from the table as he lectured on why democracy was the only system in the world that worked. He'd rant all night in order to crack Rima, dreaming of the moment she'd scream in submission, 'Yes, you're right, Mr Wax, I'm an idiot.' He would start off calmly, 'Say you have a shoe shop and I need a pair of shoes, so I come into your shop' (his visual aid was a salt shaker to represent him) 'and say "How much for the shoes?" And you' (he'd use the pepper grinder to represent Rima) 'want to sell me a pair of shoes and you say $3.00.

'Now you, Alan' (Alan Rickman would be represented by the sugar bowl) 'want the same pair of shoes. Rima, you're not going to sell me the shoes for $3.00, you're going to think, "Wait a minute." Alan' (he'd grab the sugar bowl) 'wants those shoes too. I'll charge them $6.00 or $9.00. Wouldn't you do that Rima?' he'd bark. 'And if I don't want to pay that much for the shoes, I go somewhere else.' (The salt shaker would walk away.) 'But in Russia, where nobody works, how can you sell shoes?'

Rima would then give a bit of a socialist explanation, which would open the floodgates. My father would then go into full 'Khrushchev banging his shoe on the lectern' mode climaxing with 'OK, Rima then you move to Russia where they shoot you, *up against a vall, for selling shoes!*' (The pepper would fall over.)

The bill would arrive and my father would lovingly insist that he pay because we were all 'bums with no money', then he'd happily say goodnight, having enjoyed a wonderful evening.

I was on vacation with my father in Florida a year later, when he turned to me and said abruptly, '… And another thing you can tell that Rima. If she thinks she can have a shoe shop and just give the shoes away, then she's living in a fairy world. She thinks that women should have as many children as they want and we should pay for it? Let Rima move to Russia and starve to death. See how she likes that.'

The reason I always asked Alan to come with us to dinner is that he continuously, over the years, attempted to justify my existence to my father. We had known each other since I was at the RSC and the same conversation repeated itself into my forties.

My father to Alan: 'How's she doing?'
Alan: 'Mr Wax, she's a success.'
My father: 'Says who? She's a bum.'

Sometimes they'd leave it at that. My parents pretended to have never heard of any films Alan starred in: why would a successful screen actor be friends with me? It didn't make sense. As a stage actor he was obviously some kind of loser, but a movie star? It was impossible. They vaguely heard of *Die Hard*, but would always get Bruce Willis's name wrong.

My father: 'Who vas in dat? Dat Walt Vitman?'
Alan: 'Bruce Willis, Mr Wax.'
My father: 'Never heard of him.'

Alan was once in a film that didn't do well at the box office and my parents homed in on it like vultures around a corpse. I've never seen them so happy. Alan made a strange cowboy film in Australia called *Quigley Down Under*. My father went out of his way to see it and then shot his first arrow when he met with Alan.

My father: 'Hey, Alan ... I saw that Qviggly Viggley, boy did that have the vorst reviews.'

Alan: 'Thank you, Mr Wax, I know.'

My father: 'I've read reviews but those were the vorst.' (He waited a beat.) 'The vorst. Berta, have you ever read vorse reviews?'

My mother: 'They vere the vorst.'

They worked as a team of snipers and kept the volley going for four hours. Even when the conversation went to other topics, they'd return with, 'Hey, did you ever read vorse reviews, Berta?'

Berta: 'Never. Those were the vorst.'

Father: 'I mean, I've read reviews but there are no vorse.'

Mother: 'Those vere the vorst reviews, I ever read.'

Two weeks later, my mother is saying goodbye to Alan and it

jumped from her throat like vomit, '*The vorst.*' Like that disease Tourette's, the assault kept coming.

For the two weeks they always stayed in London, they'd come to the house from first thing in the morning to late at night. As usual they did not let me do anything else. If I had to go to work I'd get:

Father: 'OK, then, go. Doing that kook stuff is obviously more important than your father.'
Mother: 'Your Highness is too busy to see the only person on earth who really cares about her.'

When I had the kids, he would throw in an extra grenade with, 'You should stay home with your kids.' When they'd come first thing in the morning, my dad would say, 'What's new?'

What could be new? I'd just have left him last thing at night. 'I brushed my teeth.'

During the day, he'd ask to see a video of my work. I'd put it on the TV and hide while he sat stony-faced, watching my various interviews. You could feel the resentment pour over him. At the end, he would ask if the BBC was happy with me, like there was a teacher grading me. He had predicted when I was a child I would fail and things weren't working his way now that I was on a major channel. At the same time he was also proud of me but didn't know how to express it. This conflict in him gnawed away and could only be released aggressively. It was easier when I wasn't around. He would constantly make me send him newspaper articles about myself which he'd show to neighbours, bank tellers, parking attendants, golf partners, anyone – but in front of me he could only abuse.

We were locked in competition. I remember I got a job in an American mini series so I told him to cancel his forthcoming visit to London. From the end of the phone I got, 'Of all of the millions of people why would they choose Ruby Wax? Thousands of girls want to act and they choose you?' When we spoke again he told me he called NBC in Los Angeles (he probably spoke to the main operator there). He said, 'I called NBC and asked if Ruby Wax was working for them – they never heard of you.'

Another time I was on *The Tonight Show* hosted by Jay Leno, which is the most popular talk show on American television. When I told him I was going to be on it so maybe he'd watch, he said, 'Which Tonight Show?'

He used to cut out articles about Tracey Ullman's success in the US and send them to me, her yearly salary circled in red felt tip.

One day out of the blue, he phoned and said, 'Boy, I just read about that Frick and Sahara [he meant French and Saunders but spitefully as usual got the pronunciation wrong]. Boy, oh boy, are they raking it in.' He claimed he read an article that stated how much they were making. 'So,' I said spitting with venom, 'why would they make more than me?' and he spat back, 'Because there's two of them.' Again, you can't argue with that.

When they got older and visited me in London, they stopped wanting to go out altogether. My father just wanted me to sit beside him as he watched CNN endlessly. My mother roamed the house bent over like Quasimodo, hunting for dust molecules. She seemed like a permanent pool cleaner. When I'd remark on her posture, she'd shriek, 'Are you crazy? I have beautiful body. I'm looking for a penny on the floor.' Even more macabre, she wore five-inch high heels. Her body was like an old question mark.

When he wasn't watching TV, my father would nap in my bed, which I found eerie. Three years ago, on one of their last visits, their behaviour got really spooky: my mother had arrived with no luggage; she wore the dress she came in for the whole two weeks of their stay. I asked 'why no luggage?'. She screamed, 'Your father was honking on the horn in the drive-way, he wouldn't let me get ready.' I could picture what happened; she was probably on the floor, chasing that illusive dust ball, my father was in the driveway late for the flight, losing his mind. He finally just took off in frustration, my mother noticed and had to run after the departing car and throw herself into it.

I came home one night from work and in my kitchen I found my mother's head on a mountain of white foam. It appeared that she had squirted a little dry-cleaning fluid onto a dirty spot on her dress, when she realised the spot was cleaner then the rest of the outfit she just kept right on squirting until she was completely buried under the white mass – the house was filled with poisonous fumes.

The first clue that my father had gone into another realm was when I was visiting them in Evanston. I was about 34 and we went to visit Harriet Hambourger to celebrate her 60th wedding anniversary. My father's driving had become hazardous due to the fact he had stopped paying attention to oncoming traffic. The outside of the Cadillac looked like it had been shelled in Afghanistan from some of his more creative manoeuvrings. Their neighbours called to say they had seen him 'bumpercar-ing' his way down the street and they were worried my parents were going nuts. 'Going?' I asked. 'Welcome to my world.' They had seen my mother wandering down the road picking up garbage; clearly, she was now not limiting her obsessions to mere interiors, soon she would be hoovering bark off trees.

Anyway we were driving on the highway toward Harriet's and I had seat-belted myself in the back seat.

We had already done two U-turns in very busy intersections and we were going about 55mph when I noticed in the distance that the cars in our lane had stopped. 'Daddy, slow down,' I said. 'There must be an accident ahead.' He accelerated, I then screamed, 'Daddy please slow down!' He calmly put his foot back on the gas and we sped up again. My mother seemed oblivious, just staring ahead. I then knew we were going to die, so I unbuckled and threw myself over the front seat and physically wrenched his foot off the pedal and pushed it on the brakes. He pulled the car off the highway and on the shoulder, I just repeated over and over again, 'Daddy you tried to kill us.' He said calmly, 'It could happen.' I arrived at Harriet's almost out of my mind. At the party my father accused me of being hysterical and that he was joking.

There was another episode in London. I took Ed's car into a garage to have it repaired. I had just gotten out with Max and made my way in front of the car to the office, when I heard a huge explosion. I ran back and found my father had climbed into the driver's seat; he'd put the car into 'drive', accelerated and driven straight into the wall in front of him where I had just passed. The hood of the car was completely concertinaed up; my father was frozen where he sat. The repairmen tried to lift his leg off the gas pedal. The rev counter was circling wildly and some black smoke was drifting out of the engine as he kept trying to drive up the wall.

I know this all happened because he was getting senile, but why did his actions seem to involve killing me? Maybe he was right – I was getting hysterical. I then drove him home; he walked in the door and announced to Ed, 'Eddie I want you to get a new car.' Ed slumped.

Towards the end of every visit, the pressure would escalate into full battle. The tension usually began with a fairly simple request from me, not to listen in to my phone conversations. During phone calls I could hear him breathing hard and then he'd actually interrupt with, 'This is your father. Hang up now I'm only here for a short while.' After I'd hung up, I'd start to tell him, shouting of course, that I have a job, three children to support and how dare he interrupt. He would build to 'full metal jacket' ending with a frail attempt to hit me, his aim wasn't what it used to be so all I had to do was move a little and he'd swipe at air. When I'd scream how dare he hit me, he'd fluctuate between saying, 'I never hit you, it's your imagination' and 'I didn't hit you hard enough.'

My mother would ineffectually try to get us to make up but each time we'd drive to the airport in silence. The hatred was thick in the air but by the time my father boarded the flight to leave, I'd have to say 'sorry', just because I knew if he died how bad I'd feel. After they'd gone, I'd run straight to Rosalie who'd tell me to ask them not to come back again, saying it was bad for my health, but I never did. Finally, fate took over. They gradually lost both their power and control over me, not because we made peace, but because a new chapter was beginning; their final trip into dementia. It broke my heart.

When does it start, your parents' final descent towards senility? At first there is a sprinkling of incidents; a few car accidents, my mother buying adult-sized clothes for my kids, my father getting lost in London and someone bringing him home, both my parents getting lost in a department store and over the tannoy you get, 'Would Ruby Wax please come to lady's accessories, we have your parents.' Then I'd hear the odd insane remark from my mother like, 'I want to call my mother,' referring to my grandmother who'd been dead for thirty years. Or repeating, 'How's the food?' three thousand times in a row. A chilling alarm call sounds through your nervous system, telling you things are falling apart and there will be no going back. My parents' feuding, vitriolic relationship stayed as it always had been, though the stakes got higher. My mother's attacks on my father launched into the realm of fantasy. At a restaurant she began an accusation that 'The bum, your father, is having an affair with Poopie' (a friend of our family for forty years). 'She's trying to get all his money. I know what's going on. She's waiting for me to die, and then she's going to marry Dad.'

My father hid my mother's handbag, because he said she was now randomly giving away money. I think he said she made a $10,000 cheque out to the window cleaner. He also hid her passport, which made her wild as she now told me she intended to move back to Vienna. It transpired that for years she'd been stashing money in an Austrian bank in order finally to return there. This was the money the Austrian government had paid her for reparations. I tried to tell her how deranged it was, that the money they gave her for kicking her out, she was investing back in again. It was like tipping them for gassing her family.

My father constantly fired, hired and refired his accountants and lawyers, so no one knew where his money was. His biggest fear seemed to be that I would rip him off. I was in his Miami flat once, and in front of me I noticed a document covered in mustard. But when I looked more closely I realised it was his will. The will stated that when I was 58 I would receive 20 per cent of my inheritance, when I was 65 I would get 30 per cent, and when I was 70, I would get 40 per cent. I spoke to his lawyer who just threw up his hands, and said, 'I know it's insane. He's trying to control you from the grave.' We all flew into Miami and Ed and I tried to talk sense into my father, we knew we were racing with time and wanted him to sign over his power of attorney to me. Clearly he wasn't in a position to make the most accurate decisions and I was his only next of kin.

It was truly the most horrible time of my life. My mother was still in Chicago. She was supposed to fly to Miami but each day she forgot where she was supposed to be going. The neighbours called to tell me they found her wandering in the street again. When I spoke to my mother, she said there were 'oodles of planes', so what's the difference which one she got on, but when I mentioned she wasn't getting on any plane so how did she plan to get to Florida? she said, 'I'll swim.' When she arrived she looked like a death mask, and her body shook from fear and atrophy.

In the end I screamed so much there were polyps on my larynx. I told my father I wanted to help him with his life, that he should sell the house in Chicago and they should move to a home. I told him he should stop using the car, as he was a driving time bomb. His hearing aid was constantly broken or perhaps he chose to shut it off, so I had no choice but to scream my advice. The only response I'd get was: '*What?*'

One day we tried to amuse the kids with a trip to Parrot Jungle, which ended in disaster: we lost both parents around the flamingo cage. I found my mother at Sea World, talking seriously to a sea-cow, Ed discovered my father absorbed in a special performance by a parakeet on a motorcycle. Young kids, senile parents … I didn't know where to look first.

All of my kids got sick in Miami, but it was my parents who demanded our complete attention and it was impossible to have a day off without them. One night Ed and I pretended we were going to bed, but really we snuck out to a club. This was the power of my father – that he could reduce people in their forties to naughty children.

It was Ed who almost got him to sign the power of attorney over to me, then just at the last moment, my father started yelling that I was planning to rob him blind and put him in a dog house. He insisted he wanted to see a lawyer. Across town my mother was in her bank, hunched over, her arms flapping wildly, howling, 'I'm a genius accountant, and my daughter is a moron. I know where every penny of my money is, but my daughter thinks I'm an idiot, she thinks I'm losing cheques. What am I? A cripple?' She was trying to light up a cigarette, only it wasn't in her mouth. Ed tried to reassure her that I was only trying to help, my mother exhaled, taking another drag of her pen, 'I don't need her help; I did everything without anyone's help.'

The last time I saw both my parents standing somewhat independently was in December 1998. I was in Chicago, to interview Jerry Springer and film backstage. The premise was I pretended to be a researcher on the show so I was asked to give a little pep talk to the guests who were transsexuals. Their secret was that they had never informed their partners they were really men. I told them something like, 'There's no business like show business ...' and sent them on stage. After the male partners tried to choke the transsexuals to death after they were informed of the 'secret', they stormed off the show, and I ran after them with my camera. I knocked on their dressing room door, pleading, 'Surely if you loved Simone, a penis shouldn't get between you. It was only a little thing. I mean you didn't notice it for three years. Can't you get over it?' The door opened; they said they could and I made everyone hug and make up. So that was successful but the next excursion wasn't.

As soon as I was done filming, I drove to nearby Evanston to negotiate with my parents. This was more difficult. I'd been told that my father had just escaped from the hospital after having a stroke. His doctor informed me that my father got so violent, he was able to fight his way out of the building. My father had been worried about my mother, who was alone and unable to take care of herself. The doctor told me my father would fail any test of sanity and that if he didn't take his medication for thinning the blood he would have a massive stroke within weeks. He also told me what I knew, that if my father got behind the wheel of a car, he would probably kill someone. When I got to our house, I begged my father to return to the hospital, he told me he'd just bought a new gold Cadillac, and was planning to drive to Miami.

I wanted to be granted guardianship, so I got someone from social services to access their mental stability, but my parents faked being normal so well, the woman said, they were still too lucid for me to take over. My mother told her, 'No thank you we don't need any help, knock on wood, I never needed a doctor, and I never will.' The once meticulous house on the lake was covered in filth and spider webs, my mother had no food in the house and her toenails were so long it looked like she had antlers on her feet.

While we were at a restaurant one night, a young guy who had done some stockbroking work for my dad happened to come by the table. My father clearly admired this guy, so I asked him loudly if he thought my father should give me his power of attorney. The guy said, 'Sure,' and my father signed it over, just like that.

A week later Ed, my kids and I were staying in the Seychelles over Christmas, compliments of Condé Nast. I was meant to write an article on a five-star luxury hotel that had recently opened, but after a 17-hour flight and sick-making helicopter ride, we found an unfinished, dangerous, nightmare. For £1,600 a night you got exposed electric wires, raw concrete, a murky green pool and a barren villa in total darkness. The empty restaurant had run out of food and wine. The next day we escaped to another island. From here I managed to phone my parents and traced my father to a Miami hospital room. There, my mother informed me, he'd had a massive heart attack and that he was having trouble speaking, but 'Knock on wood, Dad will be OK.' Just as the doctor had predicted, my father had collapsed and was now paralysed.

When my father came on the phone and his speech was slurry, I cried.

The doctor told me to come right away. We got the first available flight to London. So five days later, and after dropping the kids at home, Ed and I went straight back to the airport to fly to Miami.

When I got to Mount Sinai, I found my father tied to the bed in his room, my mother cradling his head and speaking German to him. When I asked about the restraints, I was told my father has been trying to punch out the nurses and that's when I got my first whiff of how America treats its old people. In this hospital, which costs thousands a day, I found out someone had stolen my father's false teeth and hearing aid. Such is the beauty of free enterprise, I want to tell my father, but it's now too late, his brain has gone. The doctors say inside he is thinking, but has no facility to express his thoughts. This must be what hell is like. I became the avenger my father always was. I go to the President of Mount Sinai and threaten if my father doesn't get his teeth back, I'll make a documentary about this shitty hospital as I work for the BBC. Miraculously, new teeth appear, alongside a new hearing aid.

Then I receive a call from the Cadillac dealership. It seems my father had paid for only the first month and they demand full payment for the car. I say my father's just had a stroke; he won't be needing the car. They say, tough luck, he signed for it, so it's his. Naively I asked, 'How could you sell a partially blind, 90-year-old man a new car?' They smile at my stupidity.

So it begins: first, the agonising process of finding my father a home, finding someone not corrupt to be his social worker, finding him nurses who won't tie him up, finding his money to pay for these things which are going to eventually clean him out. I was told by a hospital administrator that if I signed over everything my father's ever earned, the state would take over his care. I said, 'What do you mean by care?' and they took me to a state-run home. Let me tell you the deal, you work a lifetime and the American government will be happy to take your money and put you in a home that looks not dissimilar to the concentration camp you fled a lifetime ago. It was two storeys of flaking white stucco, filled with demented howling from wild-haired inmates covered in their own urine, no air-conditioning so it was stifling like the heat of hell; there was a stained cot in each room.

'Thank you America,' I wanted to say, for the kind offer you've made my father. I said my father will pay his own way.

I emptied my father's pockets and found crumpled cheque stubs. I'd had a list of his banks from many years ago that I always carried with me in case he croaked and we all know what state my mother was in. So every morning Ed and I would hit the phones, calling banks in Chicago, trying to locate my father's savings and of course we'd be greeted with American efficiency at its finest, hours and hours of those fucking recordings: 'If you are a lesbian and drive a Pontiac please press 1, if you like bananas or might have leprosy please dial 2 ...' All obstructing our path as we tried to glue together his financial situation. Finally, after two weeks, I had a picture of where his money was and saw he had enough stored away to ensure his comfort for the rest of his life, unless I stole it as he'd always feared.

I started to visit private facilities. I found a five-star retirement home, which is like a gingerbread hotel, all pink and pastels and no smell of urine, the staff are chirpy like it's a bingo parlour and Jewish musak is piped through speakers day and night. The hallways are crammed with Zimmer-framed traffic, bustling to their various activities like 'hair-combing' and 'watching soaps'. In the cafeteria the patients have lost all ties with civilisation, no etiquette just '*Give me a cookie!*' and then feuds would break out and suddenly a crazy person would spit in their friend's face.

I knew my father would love to live in one of these places.

So I paid out (with my father's money) $3,000 a month to Ocean Plaza, which charges you extra for every ingrown toenail removed and they will remove toenails even if you ask them not to. This price, if you happen to be paralysed and want to do something wild, like eat, doesn't include anyone who will feed you – you have to bring your own nursing staff. I had to get 24-hour hot and cold running nurses, which I did because I had access to his funds. If we hadn't gotten him to sign the power of attorney document in Evanston, a month earlier, he would have been thrown in the dog house like he always feared.

Even my earnings wouldn't begin to cover all this.

Meanwhile, my mother was living alone in their Miami apartment. I'd send in a steady stream of nurses to watch her, and she'd kick them out at 3:00 in the morning, calling the police and telling them they were trying to kidnap her. The neighbours in Miami phoned to say they were worried, 'About what?' I wanted to say. I finally couldn't take any more. She was like a wild banshee. I begged her to go into a home and she would scream, 'What am I old? Do I look like a cripple? Do you think I'm crazy? What am I mentally deranged?' Yes, to all of the above. So I took her to a shrink to see if I could have her committed to a home. I knew she wouldn't go in without a fight so I said the consultation was just to talk about Daddy. The shrink played along, and conversationally asked my mother how old she was. She took a long drag of her cigarette and answered, 'I may be off by a few years. Fifty-three.' He silently wrote out a prescription for medication.

I told one of my father's nurses to sprinkle the anti-depressants on my mother's food. She became passive immediately and I was able to move her straight into my father's room which cost more but not including toenail care. From the moment she moved in, she never remembered she had another home. She loves it there especially the exercise class where all you have to do is bend your wrists to the beat (I've done that class. It's fabulous). Since then she has become adorable, a whole new personality has emerged, someone I've never met before. A lifetime with a woman full of dinosaur rage was all over within two hours. Think of the life she, my father and I could have had if she had swallowed those pills 75 years earlier – it's unbearable to think about. Her toenails are clipped, her hair combed, her clothes cleaned and all for hundreds of thousands of dollars a year. A bargain.

One of my father's nurses, Jenny, kisses him and loves him like a child. I only wish he would of married this type of love-gushing woman. He wouldn't be where he is now and of course I'd be part Jamaican.

For the last four years, I've visited about five times a year. One ritual is I have the nurses wheel my parents into the parking lot, hoik them into a rental car and take them shopping to Bloomingdales; shopping for pyjamas, underwear and clothes, just like my mother did for me when I was a little girl. Then we all go out to a restaurant, the nurses pushing them in their wheelchairs and then placing bibs on them. Jenny feeds my father, and I feed Jenny, we do this as a joke but I feel strangely happy inside, like I'm doing something good. Sometimes I think I see a flicker in my dad's eyes, like he's finally proud of me. Then we pile the wheelchairs back in the car, and we drive back to the home.

Last year I was doing my one-woman show in which I talk a little about my father. Alan Rickman said I hope he doesn't die while you're doing it, because you'll never be able to say those lines. A week before the end of the run I got a call from the home, I was told my father had clinically died but they revived him and he had recovered. I never signed the Do Not Resuscitate document, so they had to save his life, I asked if I should come immediately but they said I could wait a week.

When I arrived in Florida my father was in a coma. He'd had to be transferred to a more hospital-like facility, because Ocean Plaza aren't allowed to have residents who cannot sit up. So there he was, lying in his room, tubes in his nose, Jenny crying. I was invited to hear the opinions of the various heads of departments, they all sat around me discussing my father's condition. It seemed to me they were imitating doctors they'd seen on television. I could pick out the George Clooney, the Noah Wylie and Juliana Margulies. They all agreed he was a vegetable, which I sort of expected, so I went back in his room, and shouted as loudly as I could, 'Daddy wake up.' He opened his eyes and said, 'Ruby?' Jenny fell to the floor crying. The black guy in the next bed and the family that surrounded him all started singing to Jesus about the miracle they had witnessed.

The so-called miracle occurred one year ago and he's been awake ever since then. He's on a feeding tube but he lives on and on, because of Jenny who moves him, massages him and loves him.

I finally sold their house in Evanston. In the attic I found hundreds of love letters to my mother, written before she married my father, and thousands of photographs of my mother looking like a movie star, travelling like an aristocrat to the French Riviera, Portofino, Venice and Switzerland. What a life she had, so full of hope – I found her school reports, all commenting upon how brilliant she was and I found the letters that had sponsored her to America and the passport with the red 'J' stamped on it.

There are other boxes filled with my father's documents; letters from one country after another, rejecting his request for entry – from the Australian Embassy, from the British Embassy, from Belgium, Holland, Spain and so on.

I found another document where someone wrote to the State Department Washington DC to have my father kicked out of the country. It reads:

Gentlemen:

This is to state that we have known Edward Wax <u>too</u> long, and recommend that you tie him out in front of the White House to scare off the Republican voters.

He is the fellow that has been sending our good samples out and filling his orders with junk which he buys in New York and confidentially, we hear that everything he eats goes to his stomach and his feet aren't mates.

Trusting that this is evidence enough to disqualify him as a citizen of the United States.

Yours very truly,

H.W. Townscend.

I found a sheaf of notepaper written by my mother. It is a list of complaints against my father – a record of his abuses. It's titled: 'Balance 1938–1972'. How she ran from a dictator, only to marry another.

We have to quiver at your commands otherwise we 'get hit' ... You have created an atmosphere of fear ... It was something you wanted most of all, the feeling of power, and the fear you can instil like an army commander or a Hitler ... Respect has to grow on its own ... By this lack of understanding, you have alienated our child ... All these terrible, ugly incidents that ruined our marriage ...

You are sick. If I did not have an ulcer before, I could also
have gotten a heart attack ... How can one human being
hold out forever under these sick conditions? I can't live
like this anymore ... If you need these things for your ego,
get another victim ... Frankly I don't even want to live
any longer.

In another letter she says,

... your insatiable sick drive to prove yourself as a man ...
I was hoping for a miracle that you might eventually
change. [Of me she says] It was almost impossible to raise
her and she was deprived besides of what most children see
in their homes – she never saw any love between us. The
time I pretended made her happy ... this home was a
freezer – with you ... punishing me. Maybe to show any
signs of love to your wife, might of made you feel less of a
man. As [their shrink] said you function in society beau-
tifully, up to the moment you entered your home ... I begin
to feel we don't even belong into a group of normal people
– we are a couple of freaks.

And then I find the letters I saved for thirty years from my
father to me. They are almost identical, saying in effect:

HOW DO YOU WANT ME?

*You have let us down again ... As usual you did not obey
instructions ... Ruby Wax is in trouble again ... I
thought that by now you'd have outgrown this greasy kid
stuff ... How many times do I have to warn you ...
Ungrateful brat ... no one is as lucky as you ... Sadly I
have to punish you for this ... You made me sick with your
behaviour ... You will never amount to much ... we are
plenty worried ... Sorry to see you are acting so immature
... in a few days you will reach 22 way past the time when
some sense of maturity is to be expected ... You are not
mentally equipped to sit behind a wheel ... You are no
credit to your country ... It is my duty to warn you this
sort of talk and behaviour is not getting you anywhere ...
I noticed you made four long distance calls, here we go
again ... Get properly groomed ... That's Ruby always
footloose and unstable ... I forbid you to throw my letters
in a wastepaper bin ... answer my letters properly ... We
will tolerate you but the world around you never will. ...
At 27 I hope you find time to read papers and get a
general idea about the world around you. To be able to
form your own opinion is absolutely necessary.*

And from mama:

To The Queen of Sheba! ... I have been watching your

choice of company which was not so exquisite. Together with your hangouts where you run after your friends. When you go to bed with dogs you wakeup with fleas, (and not our dog). Stop making an asshole out of yourself. These friends may send you maybe to the dogs ... These creeps of the underworld make me vomit ... No tantrums please but smile and accept facts and not fantasies ... was it a crime that I only wanted the best for you? ... Will you ever outgrow the schleppers? ... Unfortunately this is an hereditary affinity to shady people syndrome and in your case, I still do not give up hope that you outgrow it. Don't let nobodies play an important role in your life. Honey, it is my duty to point things out to you once in a while ... who else should care but your mother and tell you the truth ... You neglected your lovely figure and did not groom yourself properly. I suppose you have begun to realise that your mother was eating her heart out and why? Because I love you.

I fill 57 garage bags full of our life together and keep only a small pile.

The last thing I do is to rip out the round clock that hangs by a gold chain from our living room wall. It filled my nightmares since I was five as it banged against the wall which I thought was the thumping of my heart. I carry it to the lake and throw it into the water as hard as I can. I wail with glee as it sinks, Ed takes a photo.

Back in London, it was strange to think they were never coming to visit again. I knew if I was going to move on in life I'd have to get free of them, but I was still mean and angry; forgiveness, as yet, was out of the question.

How long can you blame your parents before people think you're a freak? A bore? 'Get over it' was blaring loudly in my brain. I knew that I'd never see, in the film of my life, the scene where I'm bent over Daddy on his death bed and he says, 'I'm sorry', I forgive him and we hug.

I always knew there was something beyond therapy. Rosalie taught me, you can control the head if you work hard enough at watching and controlling your behaviour. You can teach an old dog new tricks, but the next stage was opening of the heart. I had absolutely no clue as to what this meant. Outside of crying in *Bambi*, I wasn't really a very 'feeling' person.

But in 1992 I got the BBC to fund my personal search for this 'heart thing,' all in the name of light entertainment. The idea of the film was I'm caught in a crossfire of inner angst and I decide to go on a spiritual quest. I pick Los Angeles: (a) for comic reasons (obviously), (b) because as I say in the film, 'Just because I'm cracking up, doesn't mean I have to give up on room service.' My base will be the Four Seasons Hotel. At the beginning I meet new-age shysters galore. From the Dr

Barbara who made me marry myself on a Malibu beach to the 'wheatgrass up the rectum' school of enlightenment. But the second half of the film, I needed someone to open the floorboards and show me the next floor 'down' after therapy. My brief to myself was to go from the Woolworth's end of spirituality to the real thing, whatever that was. Despite my cynicism, I was scared that if I made the whole film a joke, I'd be kicked in the ass by karma. I chose for the end of the film, Tom Pinkston, a man who works with terminally ill children, to take me on one of his 'vision quests'. Even I could see he was a heavyweight.

It went like this: a group of volunteers came together at a Big Sur campsite. It was in a dense, Californian redwood forest and before sending us up a mountain for three days, with no food and, for me, no camera crew, Tom made us spend many hours peeling back our layers of pretention. In one of the exercises he made us give away something that meant a lot to us. I gave away my mirror – I thought at the time it was a funny thing, considering make-up was crucial to my image.

Leaving my crew behind me, I climbed high up the mountain, to an isolated place. Throughout the first day and night, my only thoughts were to do with hunger, then slowly, very gradually, I began to feel elation. I was free from my usual baggage, the critical voices in my head had stopped and there was a new sense of freedom. The open space seemed to be not just around me, but inside me. It wasn't the feeling of you against nature any more; it was more of a blend into it.

By day two, I had lost track of time; I was just 'there', staring, staring in awe for hours on end at the minutiae of the forest. At night, whereas I was terrified in the beginning, I now slept peacefully on the dirt, almost hugging it as if I couldn't get close enough. I felt that the tall trees were like anonymous parents watching over me. I imagined them strong and bent over me in the darkness, keeping me safe. I've always slept with the lights on, but now I loved the darkness and that niggling fear I have of death somewhere in me, diminished. I thought if death is like this, it's wonderful. On the last night, I was bitten on both eyes and woke up with them swollen shut. Uncharacteristically, I wasn't panicked. Even though I had narrow vision, I believed I could actually see more clearly.

The end of the retreat was to be signalled by a faraway drum. Following its sound, I crawled down the mountain and returned to the others. From the glances of the camera crew, it was clear I looked like hell. The group sat in a circle and we spoke for the first time in three days. Everyone spoke straight from the heart, with no fat, no frills. The last time I heard that tone was in the Priory. When it was my turn to speak, I had no idea where this thought came from. I said, among other things, 'God is in the details.' (It's not my line but it was appropriate.

Usually, I have to do many rewrites or rethinks when I'm in front of a camera, but this time it was spontaneous.)

Let's not be over-dramatic here. I'm not saying that after a three-day vision quest you change completely, but you develop a taste for that kind of complete honesty and that atmosphere.

Since then I've worked with someone who teaches meditation from the Brahma Kumaris World Spiritual University. No, I haven't found a new religion, because to me that would just be another bumper sticker and T-shirt. What I wanted to feel was that wide-open space again like I did at Big Sur. With meditation I can recreate that sensation – inside; the heart opens and for a moment I'm released from the usual feelings of hatred, resentment, expectations, recriminations, and I can glimpse what I'm like under all that garbage. This honest inner view ensures I never blame anyone around me for my unhappiness and frustration again. I don't want to sound like I'm sitting here now with crystals jammed in my chakras, listening to wind chimes and running with the wolves. Spirituality isn't like some Body Shop ointment that you smear all over yourself to cover the stench of your own shortcomings. It's tough work and I'm not even close yet, but I've taken the first baby step.

And without this work, what finally happened with my parents wouldn't have been possible.

The last time I visited them was on Valentine's Day. I was leaving their room for the airport and said to my father, in the spirit of the occasion, 'I love you.' My father, as you remember, is almost completely brain dead, and now he has a feeding tube in his throat. He hasn't reacted to any sensation for years. But he suddenly sat up and said, 'I love you, too.' Then he wept. I cried too, the kind you cry in dreams where the floods of tears are endless.

The swords were finally lowered and my heart opened.